AMERICAN TRIBAL TYRANNY

...how federal Indian policy secretly monies up
elected officials and forces American taxpayers
to fund all annual operating needs
of the Bureau of Indian Affairs
and 574 wealthy tribal governments

ELAINE DEVARY WILLMAN, MPA

ISBN: 978-1-60414-987-6

Published by Fideli Publishing, Inc.
119 West Morgan Street
Martinsville, IN 46151

www.FideliPublishing.com

DEDICATION

The writer of this book encountered severe vision problems recently resolved through the marvelous guidance, resources, and technology provided through the Blind and Low Vision Services Agency in Missoula and Helena, Montana. The agency takes no position on the content of this book. However, the staff of this agency has made it possible for the author to continue her writing and quality of living; she is forever indebted to their services and kindness.

ACKNOWLEDGEMENTS

I have greatly benefitted from the amazing skills of a wonderful friend and colleague, Lauralee O'Neil of Kalispell, Montana. Lauralee's contribution to this book in the form of editing, formatting and graphics is most deeply appreciated. She enriches my work and my life.

I also deeply appreciate the substantive contributions from "Other Voices" (Section 3) of this book: Pam Secord, Emida Valley, Idaho; Bruce Elliot, La Conner, WA; Karen Schumacher, Boise, Idaho; Butch Cranford, Plymouth, CA; Rick Jore, Ronan, MT; and a marvelous, but anonymous Oklahoma tribal woman.

I have also greatly valued my frequent communications with attorneys Lana Marcussen (AZ), Lawrence Kogan (NY), Ken Williams (CA), and Frank Kowalkowski (WI), all of whom are active, knowledgeable and successful litigators in the field of federal Indian policy.

Sadly, over the years I have lost — through their passing — four of my very early mentors, all of whom provided the foundation for my thirty years of research: John Fulton Lewis (VA), Philip Brendale (WA), Naomi Brummond (NE) and Jackie Allen (WA). They shall live on within my heart.

My ongoing research journey is immensely and warmly enriching, in large part because of the colleagues I have worked with along the way. My work is a daily act of love for my country, my family, tribal families, my peers and my friends.

PREFACE

Sail On! Sail On!
Oh Mighty Ship Of State!
To the Shores of Need,
Past the Reefs of Greed,
Through the Squalls of Hate...
Sail On! Sail On! Sail On!..
— Leonard Cohen

From its original construction and launch following the Revolutionary War, America's Mighty Ship of State has known almost continuously tumultuous waters, with little hope of a forever safe harbor. I cannot pretend to know the innermost thoughts of Leonard Cohen when he penned the lyrics of Democracy. I don't know if Cohen was thinking of freedom, socialism, communism or America's Constitution. What I take from his incredible lyric, however, is the ruthlessly honest description of my beloved America..."Cradle of the best and the worst...it's here they have the range and the machinery for change, and it's here they have the spiritual thirst.""

Toward the end of his song, Cohen says, *"I'm sentimental if you know what I mean...I love this country but I can't stand the scene."*

My sentiments exactly...I, too, love this country but I can't stand the scene, so it is time to raise my voice once again and do all that I can to change our country's "scene"

There is one other set of Cohen lyrics that in my view perfectly describes the American public perception of federal Indian policy: *"It's coming from the feel that it ain't exactly real, or it's real but it ain't exactly there."* The greater American public, particularly large populations on both coasts are fairly oblivious to tribal governments and reservations. Their information is pretty limited to visiting Indian casinos. The irony here is that the hated White Man is the customer base of mega-wealthy tribal casinos, but that issue is for further discussion in this book.

The overarching message to the reader is the urgent need to restore our Ship of State, our country to One Nation Under God...indivisible by the unconstitutional imposition of 574 tribal governments increasingly spreading a non-republic form of government in the majority of our fifty States. Ending tribalism as a governing system in this country will be a Herculean task across very tumultuous waters, but then so was the removal of slavery from this land, securing women's right to vote and own property, and other country-shaping paths forward. I invite the reader to put on a life jacket and join me in this journey to bring our Mighty Ship of State back to the navigational tools of the U.S. Constitution and One Nation Under God.

Elaine Willman

Note: To hear Leonard Cohen's entire song, *Democracy*, internet search: YouTube Leonard Cohen and Democracy.

Table of Contents

SECTION ONE
Really Bad Attitudes

CHAPTER 1

CHAPTER 2

CHAPTER 3

CHAPTER 4

CHAPTER 5

CHAPTER 6

SECTION TWO
Corruption, Here, There...Everywhere!

SECTION THREE
Other Voices

INTRODUCTION

A Severely Wounded American Eagle

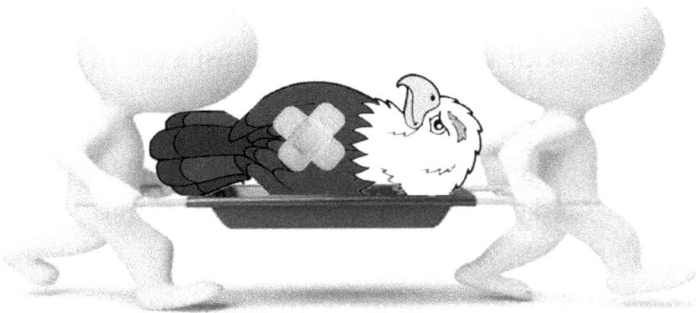

The shaft of the arrow had been feathered with one of the eagle's own plumes. We often give our enemies the means of our own destruction.

— Aesop

Some conditions never change. While Aesop lived 2,500 years ago in the 600 BC era, the simple fable messages of Aesop ring true through today. Borrowing from Aesop, our national bird, the American Eagle, is a metaphor for the internal self-destruction we citizens are doing to the United States. This introduction provides a backdrop upon which the focus of this book is occurring. The focus is on federal Indian policy. Please note that federal Indian policies are decisions made by our federal, state and local elected officials, on *behalf* of tribal governments, but not *by* tribal governments whose only authority is over its Indian trust lands and its enrolled tribal members.

For purpose of this discussion, imagine that each feather is an American citizen, and the bird is our country, the United States.

Envision the grand American Bald Eagle soaring high through bright blue skies, with a keen eye and sense of thriving over his world. That is not happening today. The bird is severely injured. Take a look at the use of the *feathers* of our country's bird that are placed into arrows with United States in the crosshairs. Here are just a few of the uses of the feathered arrows:

> ➤ Open borders — come one, come all, no vetting.
> ➤ Taxpayer fund the costs of all Illegal immigrant basic needs.
> ➤ Position the U.S. as a country that sanctions baby-killing.
> ➤ Elect U.S. officials committed to anti-American Islam at all levels of U.S. government.
> ➤ Implement environmental crop destruction and depopulation of lands.
> ➤ Normalize nationwide election fraud, including illegal voters and rigged voting machines.
> ➤ Push socialism/communism to replace a republic form of government.
> ➤ Ignore and continue devastating air, land and people with chemtrails, 5G, wi-fi and other fatal radiation pollutions.
> ➤ Continue promoting Diversity, the demand for segmenting American citizens into bickering groups based on race, ethnicity or religion.

➢ Educate two generations of young Americans to disdain and spurn the government and history of their country.

➢ Teach young American minds that entitlement is morally superior to achievement.

➢ Rebuke God, Mother Nature, and Adam and Eve with man's twisted thinking of crap-science Climate Change and "Gender Fluidity."

➢ Disregard the Constitution by creating a fourth "sovereignty," the establishment of 574 annually tax-funded tribal governments spreading across the land that supplant a republic form of government with ethnic collectivism/socialism.

➢ Muzzle and handcuff debate and discourse through nationwide media propaganda, "hate speech," and the public "stocks" of mainstream media and organizations such as the Southern Poverty Law Center.

➢ Promote profit and power of an acknowledged and exposed Deep State that operates in secrecy, flaunts the rule of law and hi-jacks our government and the voice of the American public.

The above is just a cursory list. My fellow Americans have become, perhaps unintentionally, enemies of our own country. Why? It is Americans receiving actual paychecks that are putting the destructive forces noted above into action. The list is not exhaustive; there's far more assaults on our country coming from globalists and American citizens who, for gainful employment, support socialism, communism and the demise of the United States.

Americans are piloting the chem-trail planes. Americans are installing the 5-G and radiation risks. Americans are paid to recruit illegal voters, work in abortion clinics, and create legislation that undermines the country. Federal employees are destroying farmers, cattlemen and our food production. American scientists are paid to mislead the public regarding such things as climate and gender. Americans are making good money doing bad things to our families, communities and country.

By 2016 the American Eagle (our country) had fallen from the sky, writhing on the ground: Food and crop production decimated; manufacturing gone; military downsized and neutralized; education converted to indoctrination and socialism; God and prayer removed from schools and public facilities; baby-killing on an upward spiral; envy, greed and entitlement replacing personal responsibility, achievement and aspiration. The country was like the eagle struck by arrows launched with its own feathers.

Somehow in 2016 enough of us *feathers,* American citizens, saw the country's trauma and elected a bold leader to rescue, restore and nurture our grand Eagle. The national bird is up off the ground, bleeding stopped, back on its perch, and healing to soar once again. Yet millions of Americans are infuriated with their rescue and rescuer.

Most of us have family members we cherish and numerous friends and colleagues we respect. Family and friends enrich our lives. We have many of these. We do all we can for them. We only have one country. One. We do all that we can for our family and friends who live here in the United States, but we do damn little for the only country we have.

We can keep silent watching as our fellow Americans continue sending fatal arrows into our country, but for our next generation many may only know the term "American" as a historical reference to a country that used to be.

Against the backdrop of the multiple conditions described above that are eroding the prosperity and liberties in our country, this book focuses on an ill-understood, little known but rapidly escalating federal push to launch an assault on state sovereign authority by pushing tribalism as a replacement form of government across this country. While all of the debilitating arrows described above can be considered temporary and capable of change, the 200-year movement to reverse history, "decolonize" America, demean all who are not native Americans, is hitting an enormous financial and political tipping point, the need to eliminate divisive federal Indian policy and all forms of ethnic diversity is the underlying cancer preventing equal opportunity for all American citizens and the restoration of One Nation Under God.

Readers will note that within the various chapters are terms that frequently reoccur. This is intentional because: 1) the terms are fundamental to the subject discussed within each chapter; and 2) we learn by repetition and need to become well-educated about federal Indian policy terms to better communicate with our elected officials.

Those who grew up believing in the United States, grateful for liberty and freedom must engage in daily efforts to keep the American Eagle soaring. Old Aesop and 2,500 years of nation births and deaths reflect what happens to countries that self-mutilate and destruct. Like another newer adage: if we snooze, we lose. My hope is that this book is a major alarm clock. It's time to wake up!

SECTION ONE

Really Bad Attitudes

THE TEN CANNOTS

In 1916, a minister and outspoken advocate for liberty, William J. H. Boetcker, published a pamphlet entitled "*The Ten Cannots*" that fittingly contrasts the competing political and economic factions today:

1. You cannot bring about prosperity by discouraging thrift.

2. You cannot strengthen the weak by weakening the strong.

3. You cannot help the poor man by destroying the rich.

4. You cannot further the brotherhood of man by inciting class hatred.

5. You cannot build character and courage by taking away man's initiative and independence.

6. You cannot help small men by tearing down big men.

7. You cannot lift the wage earner early by pulling down the wage payer.

8. You cannot keep out of trouble by spending more than your income.

9. You cannot establish security on borrowed money.

10. You cannot help men permanently by doing for them what they will not do for themselves.

THE TEN CANNOTS

'It's easier to fool people than to convince them that they have been fooled.'

— Mark Twain

CHAPTER 1

An Open Letter to Navajo Nation Chairman Russell Begaye

"For Native Americans this (America) is our land. Every inch of it, every mountain, every stream, every water that is out there is ours. It's Native American country... America is Indian Country, and so every non-Indian out there is a guest of Native Americans in this country' and that's how they should act, so if you're a guest in our country that's how you should act." (Navajo Nation President, Russell Begaye, Nov. 28, 2017, live on CNN)

https://www.cnsnews.com/video/navajo-nation-president-every-non-indian-out-there-guest-native-americans-country

Dear Russell,

I have had to settle my feelings down for days to even start this letter. Your November 28, 2017 comments on CNN hit my Last Straw Button.

As one who has cherished my family's Indian ancestry and the colorful, proud and rich history of all Native Americans, I found myself conflicted with an ongoing desire to continue this respect, torn apart when you spit in the face of every fellow American, me included. Worse, your condescending statement renders the United States wrong from its origin, assumes the non-existence of the United States and would render the voice of all other Americans irrelevant and silent. Every federal dime your tribal government has annually received from American taxpayers since the early 1800s to the present time should therefore be returned to the *guests* who have never owed you anything, in the first place.

All the economic benefits, schools and colleges, the technology conveniences of electricity, automobiles, medical equipment, flat-screen TV's, cell phones, laptops, slot machines—must necessarily be discarded from "Indian Country" lands as these life-enhancing products created by other cultures are non-Indian *clutter* created by the *guests* you hold in such disdain.

Historically since the growth of this still very young United States, American Indians are the only ethnicity to receive ongoing federal support: tax-exempt land and businesses, annual funding, and special preferences of every stripe. As example, when America was only sixty-six years old in 1855; five years even before the Civil War and throughout major Wars and international threats, conditions on the ground across America were as follows:

> ➤ In 1855 President Franklin Pierce sent Washington Territory Governor Isaac Stevens across the West to execute Treaties with Indian tribes, that paid cash for land, created private and protected

land spaces for Indians, provided annual dollars, blacksmiths, schools, doctors, etc. for American Indians.

➤ In 1855 after the earlier Louisiana Purchase the Presidents and Congress were saying "Go West Young Man" to settle and develop the continental United States. Young man was given absolutely nothing from the federal government, except a hope. Young Man put what he had in a wagon, headed to the unknown, staked out and built a homestead, then more homesteads, then roads, schools, churches, communities…Young Man built the West and this amazing United States with rugged individualism and zero charity from the federal or any government.

➤ In 1855, two years before Harriett Beecher Stowe's *Uncle Tom's Cabin*, Black Americans were still being bought, sold and used as cattle, not even considered human. It would be over another hundred years before Black Americans even received Civil Rights and segregation was brought to its knees.

➤ Before and long after 1855, immigrants from all countries coming to America were welcomed, were provided nothing and were expected to contribute to the young growing United States by first respecting its very existence and unlimited blessings, values and laws.

The only residents of this country to constantly receive bounty, annual beneficial assistance, protections, cash payments for lands, race-based special preferences is…yep, folks like you, Russell, who continue to stick a thumb in the eye to this country and its people that sustain you. I have never heard the Native American word for "thank you," or perhaps, "Enough." All I hear is disgust and disdain for all other cultures… and Give Us MORE.

Here's the irony: All the annual billions of dollars over two centuries, land and benefits enjoyed by now 574 tribal governments in the United States are directly and solely from the goodness of the Heart of the American People and those they elect. No such benefits or even tribal government existence is contemplated in America's U.S. Constitution. The Constitution provides no preference to who was here first or last. The Constitution requires compensation (no takings) for lands (i.e. all treaties, Louisiana Purchase of 1803, Gasden Purchase 1853, Alaska Purchase 1867).

There is not a single word or text within the four corners of the U.S. Constitution where its Framers ever contemplated the existence of tribal governments in the United States. Not one word. Everything Indian tribes receive from the United States is outside of the U.S. Constitution, and inside the Good Heart of America's *guests*. In the 1830s it was the U.S. Supreme Court (nine *guests*) that established a federal "trust" relationship with Indians, setting the stage for annual bounty and special privileges for one race. But beware, Mr. Begaye: what the U.S. Supreme Court gives, it can and may soon, also take away.

With incessant ingratitude from Indian Country, I think *guests* should be done with all that. Since at least 2004 and recently in various rulings, Justice Clarence Thomas has questioned the "Plenary" authority of Congress over Indians and tribal governments under the Indian Commerce Clause, or the Supremacy Clause. On November 27, 2017 Justice, Clarence Thomas wrote the following in an unusual and striking Dissent objecting to the High Court's failure to take up an important case:

> "…the Indian Commerce Clause does not appear to give
> Congress the power to authorize the taking of land into
> trust under the (Indian Reorganization Act) IRA. Even

assuming that land transactions are "Commerce" within the scope of the Clause....Under our precedents, Congress has thus obtained the power to take any state land and strip the State of almost all sovereign power over it "for the purpose of providing land for Indians." 25 U. S. C. §5108. **This means Congress could reduce a State to near nonexistence by taking all land within its borders and declaring it sovereign Indian territory. It is highly implausible that the Founders understood the Indian Commerce Clause, which was virtually unopposed at the founding, as giving Congress the power to destroy the States' territorial integrity**...Indeed, they would have been shocked to find such a power lurking in a Clause they understood to give Congress the limited authority "to regulate trade with Indian tribes living beyond state borders." When our precedents permit such an absurd result, something has gone seriously awry. It is time to fix our error." Justice Clarence Thomas, November 27, 2017 in Dissent against Denial of Writ of Certiorari in *Town of Vernon vs. U.S.*

https://www.courthousenews.com/thomas-outraged-in-dissent-to-oneida-land-dispute/

So why is it important that I get this message to you, Russell? Because you still have the respect of those you call *guests*. However, respect cannot be demanded. It must be earned. Your preference for apartheid, race-based governance and Indian Country blended with animosity for the United States has opened an even uglier door for this country. The tribalism of Middle Eastern countries and Sharia law is finding separatist "Indian Country" successes inviting and attractive for bringing more international tribal factions into the United States. Former President Obama and Congress have even acknowledged the common, communal and cultural similarities between American and Middle Eastern tribal cultures. The Hearth Act of 2012 now encourages partnerships with America's tribes and Turkey and Saudi Arabia. Many tribes are currently conducting leadership and student exchanges with Turkey and Saudi Arabia. See especially pages 8-9, 17-26, and 39-47 at the following link:

http://www.klamathbasincrisis.org/doi/2017/020217_RejectionofRyan ZinkeNomineeforSecretaryofInterior%20.pdf.

There is a reason the Forgotten Man that you call *guests* in America has called for massive federal change to take back this country and Make America Great Again. It is difficult to be One Nation Under God with 574 separate tribal governments within our fifty Constitutional states. When you keep kicking sand in our face, we eventually get the message. You just delivered it, front and center on CNN around the entire world. No one stole your land, there is no absolute certainty that "you were here first." Life changed for all of us on September 17, 1789 with the formation of the United States Constitution government. I was born in 1943 in Portland, Oregon. I am as *native* and *indigenous* to the United States as an American citizen as you are—no more, no less. The United States of America is not Indian Country.

Most sincerely,

Elaine Willman,
Ronan, MT
toppin@aol.com

Truth is now called HATE speech. Why is that? It's because during times of universal deceit, telling the truth becomes a revolutionary act.

— George Orwell

CHAPTER 2

"Mom Always Liked YOU Best!"
... Federal Indian Policy

It's eighty-three years late in coming, but at long last the Indian Reorganization Act of 1934 (IRA) is finally getting its first-ever review, and hopefully serious reform. IRA (48 stat. 984) forms the backbone of federal Indian policy across the country and has been extended, expanded and abused far beyond the original intent of Congress.

In order to understand IRA and its major impacts on America, let me share an analogy. Imagine an American household with a single mom and a couple of sons, Johnny and Jimmy. One day Mom calls the family together to make an announcement.

"Johnny, you were here first; Jimmy you were here second. Therefore, Johnny, you are more valuable and important than your brother. And Jimmy, you have intruded upon Johnny's room, his life and his world, so a big chunk of everything you earn from now on and forever will be given to me, Mom, and I will redirect your earnings to Johnny. You really don't belong here, Jimmy, because you were here second."

This is exactly what has been happening in our country for eighty-three years. Since the Tribes (Johnny) tell the government (Mom) that they were here first, the non-tribal Americans (Jimmy) have become second-class citizens. Few parents would prioritize a preference for one child over another. Our federal government, however, is doing exactly that: assigning preference for one American ethnicity over another.

The mantra foisted upon Americans for decades is, "We were here first; you stole our land." Neither is true. But even if it were true, the response as of 1789 should have been, "So what?" That was the way of the world in the 1600's under the Doctrine of Discovery. Life changed on this continent in September 1789.

One could hardly call the poor souls arriving on the Mayflower and other ships to establish a new life on this continent, conquerors. They had fled religious oppression under a tyrannical King, and were seeking liberty, religious and individual freedom. These were the seeds that became the Great American Experiment. But for that "transgression," apparently, Americans are to be forever damned.

In my analogy, Mom is our Mother Country. Imagine that Mom's folks come to visit their grandsons and discover the new household rules. Mom's folks, representing our Founders, would be astonished. The seeds planted in the early 1600s by arrivals from Europe gave birth to the Framers of our Constitution, and our Republic form of government. Regardless of historical decisions, some right, some wrong, the reality is that the United States of

America, as of September 1789, is our government, inclusive of the now fifty separate and sovereign states. Revisionist history has been common practice for far too long, but the actual reversal of history occurring today is the slumbering thunder creeping across this country.

There is no tribal sovereignty recognized in the U.S. Constitution, but such sovereignty (just like Jimmy paying perpetual debt to Johnny) has acquired a power beyond the Constitution's declared sovereign authority of individual citizens and states. States like Washington, Montana, Idaho and some Midwestern states have continually relinquished their state authority in deference to all tribal whims. Many states have created *de facto* "trust" relationships with tribes where none were required or existed; only the federal government has a court ordered (but not constitutional) "trust" relationship with their individual "dependent wards—NOT Indian tribal governments."

As of May 2000, Johnny's governments (tribes) may directly finance political parties, incumbents or candidate election officials. Jimmy's governments may not. Johnny's businesses are all tax-exempt and growing enormously. Jimmy's businesses are taxed to the max. Johnny's government members can hold elected office anywhere across the country, passing land use and taxation laws upon Jimmy that do not apply to Johnny. Johnny has priority over most of the river and water systems throughout the Western states because Johnny was here first, and Jimmy's needs don't matter...he shouldn't exist.

There is a wondrous Statue of Liberty in New York harbor that welcomes all to come, as the early Jamestown settlers, legally to the United States. We are a country forged and thriving by "intruders" from all over the world. Our republic form of government does not classify those who were here first as superior, nor does it distinguish a priority between the person naturalized yesterday as a full American citizen and the child born here five minutes ago. But federal Indian policy requires perpetual debt and shame for all who came second.

And now we take a deeper look at the Indian Reorganization Act and its impact on the lives of American citizens. In 2009, the U.S. Supreme Court ruled in *Carcieri v Salazar* that IRA was intended to *reorganize* **only those tribes on existing reservations and "now under federal jurisdiction" in June 1934.**" There were only some 65-70 actual Indian reservations in the United States in 1934. Therefore, the IRA was to *reorganize* only those 65-70 tribes, and no more. The *Carcieri* ruling was a political earthquake.

The Department of Interior and Bureau of Indian Affairs have not just reorganized reservations in existence in 1934; they have federally recognized a current total of **574** tribal governments, each acquiring and expanding their reservations, each receiving tax exemptions, and each receiving annual operational money from Jimmy ("second-class" citizens).

The response to *Carcieri* under the Obama administration was to utterly ignore it, along with other Supreme Court rulings where the High Court rolled back tribal governing authority, replacing state sovereign authority.

The good news is that on June 22, 2017, the Department of Interior published a "Notice of Regulatory Reform" with an open public comment period on the Indian Reorganization Act (IRA) and four other major federal statutes. The Notice reads:

> "This document also provides an overview of Interior's approach for implementing the regulatory reform initiative **to alleviate unnecessary burdens placed on the American people…"**

No doubt Johnny's 574 tribal governments and the entire Indian industry will be weighing in with their comments to legitimize and further expand decades of IRA unauthorized overreach.

This was our very first opportunity to truly confront the erroneous and detrimental policies that one ethnicity that was here "first" is superior to all others in this country because all other ethnicities are intruders on this continent, and that communalism, socialism and tribalism is preferable to individual liberty and a republic form of government.

It is imperative that states, counties, towns, and Jimmy—who lives within an Indian reservation—describe their "burden" at this time. If Jimmy stays silent, Jimmy's wallet will continue to be annually poached for the expansion of tribalism as a governing system, replacing our Constitutional republic form of government.

Comments can still be submitted on the record to the Department of Interior in one of two ways:

1. Submit comments to the federal *"eRulemaking Portal,"* www.regulations.gov. In the Search box, enter the appropriate document number (**DOI-2017-0003-0002**). or,

2) Mail a hard copy of your comments to: Office of the Executive Secretariat, ATTN: Reg. Reform; U.S. Department of Interior; 1859 C Street NW. MailStop 7328; Washington, DC 20240.

All other Americans are up against 574 tribal governments with 400 more "tribes" waiting in the wings for their recognition (*not* "reorganization"). How long must Jimmy owe his older brother who was here "first" and who seldom says "thank you," and never says "enough"?

I am not a second-class American citizen. Are you?

"The mind once enlightened cannot again become dark."

— Thomas Paine

CHAPTER 3

Kneecapping America with "Yesterday Sticks"

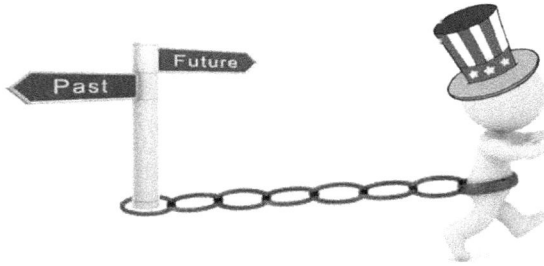

One of the most mean-spirited emotional weapons is what I call the *Yesterday Stick*. Here's how it works: A long-time married couple has survived a long-ago spousal affair, but one spouse never forgets and raises that *Yesterday Stick* as a power tool frequently in their marriage. Or a recovering alcoholic has successfully turned his/her life around with several years of sobriety, but relatives continually remember that "we knew you *when...*!" Or a convicted felon who has paid the consequences and transformed his/her life is forever stained with the *Yesterday Stick*.

Yesterday facts are unfortunate events that cannot be changed. Slavery is one. Tribalism is another. Black Lives Matter radicals rely upon the *Slavery Stick* to continually demean all of America's ancestors and founders. Our country stopped this madness over a century ago, but weaponizing yesterday's flaws today works marvelously to spread false guilt and inferiority to our fellow Americans in this and future centuries. Until we stop it. Just stop it.

The same can be said for long-ago dead Indian treaties. The legal industry thrives on conflict, so asserting ancient Indian treaty rights in the present creates instant conflict in light of contemporary demographics, towns and counties on reservations today. It also fuels a ton of money to legal firms willing to argue anything for a buck. The Washington State *"Culvert"* case in front of the U.S. Supreme Court was a prime example. The case asserts that old treaty rights are superior to state sovereignty. Yet, life has dramatically changed with predominantly non-Indian populations on reservations that include state, county and municipal jurisdictional authorities within reservation boundaries. Tribal constitutions limit their governance to their enrolled members and their Indian lands, only. That's likely why tribal governments and the legal industry are rapidly reclaiming old dead treaty rights for off-reservation and "aboriginal" rights.

On most reservations it is the non-Indian economy that provides abundant resources and quality of life to tribal and non-tribal reservation residents. And yet, the growing trend of reasserting treaty rights sends a message that all Congressional statutes and judicial rulings from the 1850's forward are irrelevant, and that only treaty rights are perpetual and cannot be supplanted. What a whopper of a lie is this *Yesterday Stick*.

Perhaps the remedy is to actually acknowledge these treaty rights and remove all *other* benefits that Congress and communities have provided to tribal governments for 200 years. Restore reservations to the 1850's — no more annual funding to tribes, no electricity, no flat screen TV's, no cell phones, no cars, no casinos, nothing that non-tribal Americans created for the benefit of all. Return reservations to their Old Life Ways under their old dead treaties. Yes, were we to succumb to the Treaty *Yesterday Stick*, the irony is that the resulting lifestyle would be one Native Americans truly would not want today. Instead, we have heavily rewarded tribal government with ongoing largesse while getting sand kicked in our teeth.

Justice Antonin Scalia in agreement with Justice Clarence Thomas, have clearly described America's racial problem in a 1995 Indian law Supreme Court ruling as follows:

> *"More than good motives should be required when govern-ment seeks to allocate its resources by way of an explicit racial classification system…the basic principle of the Fifth and Fourteenth Amendments to the Constitution protects persons, not groups…distinctions between citizens solely because of their ancestry are by their very nature odious to a free people."* — Adarand v. Pena, USSC (1995)

We are clearly not a free and equal people while racial classifications exist in any form in America. We will never be a free people while American taxpayers are indentured to annually subsidize all the basic needs of just one ethnicity — 574 Native American tribal governments.

So how are these *Yesterday Sticks* implemented? Within Columbia Law Professor Philip Hamburger's acclaimed body of expertise on Administrative Law in America, we learn that the Executive Branch has created a power-ful workaround that transfers power from Congress and the Courts to fed-eral "regulatory" agencies. There is no better example than the enormous Bureau of Indian Affairs, staffed by thousands of predominantly tribal employees, funding all basic needs of 574 tribal governments composed of a mere 0.06% of our country's population. Yet another example is the thug-gery implemented upon landowners across the country by Environmental

Protection Agency, the Bureau of Land Management, U.S. Fish and Wildlife, U.S. Department of Agriculture, et al.

Each of these federal agencies has their own Administrative Law Courts. They make the rules, set the fines and penalties, impose and enforce their regulations upon persons and private properties (bypassing state authority), then stand as judge and jury when a citizen objects. The Interior Board of Indian Appeals is a prime example of an agency Administrative Law Court. Imagine any objectivity in such a court. Federal agency autonomy, coupled with their administrative law courts, is a debilitating system that far exceeds the intent of the balance of power between the three branches of government and States succinctly defined in the U.S. Constitution.

In addition to Administrative Law, there is the onslaught of the Diversity Principle, fueled by 156 separate ethnicities identified by the U.S. Census Bureau, each category of which sets the stage for racially- based funded programs. Diversity propaganda over the past decade has turned "Equality" into an undesirable term…now politically incorrect. Americans are consistently categorized by skin tone in a racial hierarchy that trumps our Constitutional Amendments and puts equality six feet underground.

The entrenchment of these racial *Yesterday Sticks* is such that their removal from our American governance would be an earthquake shift among federal and state agencies, but it can and should be done. Just suppose that all federal funding was based solely upon one single and neutral requirement—annual household income. Period. Annual household income would not involve race, religion, marital status, sexual lifestyle; nothing except household income. It would simply be a calculation of the number of citizens within an American household, and an established poverty income threshold level. That simple. Such fairness would collapse race-based programs throughout the maze of federal and state agencies, including the Bureau of Indian Affairs. The simplicity of Annual Household Income would eliminate most, if not all, of the *Yesterday Sticks*, and restore the principle of equality to its rightful place in this country. No American household in poverty would be ineligible.

Remedy will not come easily, but could begin with an Executive Order that requires elimination of all race-based federally funded programs within a reasonable time; perhaps two to three years. Congress could then follow the lead of the Executive Branch and ensure that America ceases its racial preference funding.

Tribalism is communalism based upon race and was never contemplated as a governing system in the U.S. Constitution. Communalism is socialism, antithetical to the government our Founders provided. The federal government should return back to the tribes all lands acquired by tribes and donated to the federal government to be held in "trust" title by the United States on behalf of Indian tribes. Tribally owned lands should be restored to the authority and jurisdiction of the state, like all other lands ceded to the states upon statehood.

The severity of tribalism and diversity *Yesterday Sticks* is truly kneecapping equality and individual civil rights in this country. It is not too late to end these debilitating forces, but if nothing is done, it soon will be too late.

In the beginning of a change, the PATRIOT is a scarce man,
and brave and hated and scorned.
When his cause succeeds, the timid join him,
for then it cost nothing to be a PATRIOT."

— Mark Twain 1904

CHAPTER 4

Failure to Act
Equals Guaranteed Defeat

One of the most debilitating conditions affecting property owners in the Western states today is an entrenched core value to respect authority, to be polite, to participate in consensus, even when results cost them dearly. These values worked quite well when federal agencies shared them. They worked well when state agencies and judicial systems shared them. That mutual respect between government and the governed has almost entirely disappeared.

For too many landowners in the Western states respect has turned to fear, even anger, and for good reason. Federal agencies are now substantially armed, are militarized and have gone entirely rogue under past administrations. This condition is somewhat improving with the current federal administration (Trump) but remains a threat from federal agencies. State agencies are loath to confront this condition, and State sovereignty is the one primary shield between a hostile federal government and its citizenry. So, we landowners are essentially on our own.

Reaction to this severe political shift within the federal government has been sadly ineffective. Far too many land and business owners have responded with: 1) handwringing, whining; 2) complete paralysis, silence; and/or 3) full-on appeasement and acquiescence. For Westerners, we're becoming butterflies getting pinned live, to the mat.

Using confiscation of state waters occurring simultaneously in multiple states as example, there is a clearly discernible strategy occurring, with strikingly similar defeatist response from affected landowners.

The pattern begins with many secret years of federal policy development, then initialization of policies fully staffed and scripted to spin a benign intent to those directly affected. The tools include the Endangered Species Act, Indian federal reserve water rights, national monument policies, Clean Air and Clean Water Acts, climate change and new federal "drought resilience" programs bringing the feds right onto private properties, bypassing states.

Federal policies are more often introduced as "Done Deals," that folks can only comply with and support. The pattern includes two insidious components: 1) Getting into the local communities and instilling divisiveness among good friends and neighbors; 2) On-the-ground federal operatives masquerading as *helpers* to the locals who struggle with or directly oppose federal actions. Confusion and conflict reduce the collective voice among local folks such as irrigators, cattlemen, hunters, etc.

The Klamath (Oregon) and CSKT (Montana) areas are two examples of these patterns manifesting. Irrigators are fighting amongst themselves with appeasers confronting those who oppose a federal jackboot on their property or civil rights. Western family and friendship values are so strong that local conflict becomes too painful, so many voices go silent, with a shrugged "Oh, well, there's nothing I can do about it." This is exactly the result federal operatives intended. There is not a united voice of irrigators vigorously opposing the removal of four dams in the Northern California, Southwest Oregon area. There is not a united voice of irrigators and water users in the Flathead reservation area vigorously opposing the federal hijacking of all water and water control.

The "Oh well" folks will have dry wells and no water soon. The failure to act guarantees it. Folks in both of these areas are land rich and cash poor, another advantage for the feds and tribes. "I'd fight but I can't afford it…" So failure to act will likely cause the landowner to walk away from his valuable property, at a rock bottom price or direct forfeiture. Too often, neighbors will not enter the political dialogue because they don't want to upset their neighbors and friends.

The obvious, that authentic friends would never deny a neighbor the right and need to protect his property, is apparently not a factor.

It is very painful to study, research, inform and then watch such a sophisticated federal system take down the crop production and livelihoods in one region after another, in one state after another, when the targeted landowners stay muzzled, financially risk averse, and kind to their neighbors, even if it costs them their future on their lands. The outcome is predictable. Landowners and states lose; the feds win. State sovereign authority runs or slips away; the feds win; landowners fail to act on their own behalf; they lose the future. Doing nothing today guarantees that large areas of Americas food production in the Western states will disappear with great speed.

Our choice must be to stand up and protect Constitutional property rights in order to protect America's food production or become a country dependent upon our food sources coming from foreign countries. Is there really a choice here? I don't think so.

*"When people get used to preferential treatment,
equal treatment feels like discrimination."*

— Thomas Sowell

CHAPTER 5

Disparity Based Upon Race...
Promises Kept and Promises Broken

The 1850s were important years of growth, expansion and uncertainty for our country. *"Go West, Young Man,"* was first expressed in 1851 in the *Terre Haute Express* and later magnified across the country by journalist, Horace Greeley. By the latter 1800s the United States had acquired all the lands that now host the 48 lower states. Even with a looming Civil War, three major movements were in play — confronting slavery, managing Indian tribes and settling lands West of the Mississippi. These were difficult, competing interests for Congress to address simultaneously.

In 1852 Harriett Beecher Stowe's *Uncle Tom's Cabin* forced the American public to accept the reality that Black Americans were fully sentient human beings deserving of all the respect and opportunities of every other American. Precipitating the Civil War, Stowe's book educated the public and furthered dramatic efforts to end slavery.

Managing Indian tribes took the form of establishing Indian reservations through Congressional Acts, Executive Orders or Treaties. The intent here was three-fold: 1) to pay for ancestral Indian lands ceded to the U.S. and establish reservations for the beneficial use and occupancy of Indian tribes; 2) provide Indians with a protected area and resources for their communal living; and 3) keep separations between Indians and settlers arriving in the West. These policies provided American Indians with land, annual funds, blacksmiths, doctors, schools, commodities and other resources, and the protection of the Bureau of Indian affairs that had full jurisdiction over the Indian reservations.

Settlers hearing the call to *Go West* loaded wagons with whatever they could carry and headed into the unknown lands west of the Mississippi. The federal government, dependent upon citizens to explore and settle the new lands, provided these settlers absolutely nothing but the government's best wishes. Eventually, in 1862, Congress passed the Homestead Act, offering settlers the opportunity to stake out some land, establish a homestead and work on the land, and then, after five years, pay for that land at a reduced rate. Nothing was freely provided; everything required the courage, endurance and sweat equity of pioneer families settling the west. These hardy souls built small homes, farms, ranches, local schools, churches and towns, and the West started reflecting the Rugged Individualist that answered the call to Go West. This ultimately led to the building of Seattle, Sacramento, San Francisco, Los Angeles, etc.

Over time American Individualists and their descendants of all ethnicities built railroads, automobiles, ships, electricity, telephones, aircraft and numerous other inventions for the efficiency of homes, farms, schools and businesses. When Congress determined that a better lifestyle for American Indians would be their right to full citizenship and assimilation it passed the Dawes Act of 1887, opening the Indian reservations to all things created by settlers and for the equal benefit of American Indians.

Today all Americans, including enrolled Indians on reservations may enjoy all the resources of American productivity. This is in addition to the continued annual resources provided by the federal government to tribal governments. Massive funding to tribal governments seldom trickles down to upgrade the quality of life on Indian reservations. Tribal funds primarily disappear into an unaudited sinkhole, unavailable to assist its tribal members.

There is a sharp distinction, however, between attitudes of tribal families across the country that are generally quite separate from the 'Indian Industry.' Tribal families are good neighbors and appreciative of modern conveniences. The 'Indian Industry' is entirely focused on political power and money and can be defined in large part as the national gaming industry, national tribal organizations, the legal profession and lobbyists.

It is this national propaganda of the 'Indian Industry' megaphone that constantly slathers guilt, shame and disgust about most everything non-Indian. American productivity is offensive and obviously not working, if one listens to the mantra of the 'Indian industry' that proclaims: *We Were Here First, You Stole our Land, All of America is Indian Country, We Are Victims of White Supremacy*, etc.

Apparently, if we are to believe the long-term propaganda goals of national tribal leaders, American Indians would rather return to a hunter/gatherer culture that lives without any life-enhancing productivity provided by American settlers and their descendants. They want all non-Indians to go away from the continent and the United States as a country to disappear. They want their Old Life Ways. **Seriously**? And what productivity, inventions, conveniences, practices have tribal governments provided to their members or to the rest of the country? Do tribes really want to return to warring with each other as they did for hundreds of years before and after the first Pilgrims arrived?

By 1924, when Congress passed the Native American Citizen Act, all American Indians were made full citizens. At this point, because the United States does not execute treaties with its citizens, all treaties were de facto nullified. Tribal governments and reservations should have then been dissolved, while American Indians most certainly could have continued their customs and cultures as they desired, wherever they lived, the same as other cultures still do.

What we have as a continuous conundrum for Congress is a special-preference racial entity that annually demands and takes ever-increasing resources from American taxpayers and provides nearly zero in return. This expansion of tribalism *in perpetuity* is driven by the money and power-mongering Indian Industry that literally purchases elected officials to do their bidding.

Equally as important, tribal nations proudly proclaim the philosophy of far-sighted thinking for Seven Generations. If the incessant demands to undo the United States and its people were to succeed, it is quite possible that less-friendly, less-generous world countries would immediately step into the shoes of the disappeared United States and decimate American Indians within One Generation.

Promises have been amply fulfilled for tribal governments, whether (and generally, not!) this largesse is distributed among tribal families. Promises made to those non-tribal citizens who built this country were almost non-existent, except for those required by our U.S. Constitution. The expansion of resources and power for 574 tribal governments now threatens the republic form of government for all non-Indians residing within Indian reservations as promised by the Homestead Act and Dawes Act. Today's Rugged Individualists need to pay attention now more than ever and push back on this governing slippage.

So here is a challenge: Perhaps national and local tribal leadership could consider a change of attitude that would include cooperation, appreciation and intentionally sought harmony among ***all*** people in this country.

Would a different world government treat tribal governments better? Having received the continuous bounty of this country, and contributed little in return, perhaps a bit of gratitude should be considered. What is wrong with **all** American citizens mutually respecting one another? Regard for our respective cultures is simply the right thing to do.

Why must taxpayers of every ethnicity annually fund, for *"time immemorial,"* **one** ethnicity over all others—an ethnicity whose powerful national voice foments such disparaging of the United States and its citizens?

It is a hard, undeniable truth that the federal government cannot
give to anybody what it does not first take from somebody else,
and the power to do so is ruinous.
As Thomas Jefferson wrote, we must "prevent the government from wasting
the labors of the people, under the pretense of taking care of them."

— Anonymous

CHAPTER 6

My American Homeland

D uring the Vietnam War years I owned a lovely home on Stonybrook
Drive in Anaheim, California. My children's learning, memories,
family traditions and life-experiences were forged in that home. My
children were native to that soil. Although we had to move away and have
been gone for many years, it was the ancestral homeland of our family origins.

Recently I realized how deep our family roots were in that Stonybrook
home; our ancestral, indigenous origins, so to speak. I sorrowed over the loss

and the need to recover that piece of history for my family's future seven generations to come. So, I wrote the current owners, and explained the importance of that property to my family. I told them we were there first, wanted the home back, asked them to send me the title and make plans to move out.

They told me to buzz off. A deal is a deal. And they were right to do so under our Constitutional government, federal and state property laws. That is the case for all citizens in this country. A deal is a deal; you move on with time.

Not so for American Indians.

Today, tribal voices inform our federal and state officials that their ancestors once walked through our forests, fished in our rivers, hunted in our hills, and they want their lands back for their seven generations to come. They assert aboriginal and time immemorial rights that pre-date the formation of the United States Constitution, government and country. They write letters to federal officials like I did to the current Stonybrook homeowners. The federal and state officials say, "Oh my, you're right, we'll get that land right back to you; we'll move off current private landowners, we'll deny American citizens the right to hunt and fish where you do; we'll turn our national forests over to you for tribal management and hiring practices. Oh, and our taxpayers will keep funding all your tribe's basic life needs forever, give you a monopoly on tax-exempt gambling, and allow *your* governments to be the only governments in the United States that can contribute money to candidates and political parties in our elections. You can buy our elected officials too, to give you even more. What else can we do for you?"

Oh, here's more. In 2010 Congress passed the Indian Energy Policy Act, opening up the country's power grid to tribes, and funded billions for tribal governments to take over dams, water, utility and electric power systems across the country. Never mind that tribal governments have no duty to the utility customer base. Tribes cannot be sued nor is any previous experience required. But no matter! Need more? In 2012 Congress said tribes could long-term lease their federal trust lands to "religious" (Middle Eastern) countries. They have tons of money and want to position themselves across the U.S.—so that is another great opportunity.

This is exactly how aggressive tribal leaders of 0.5% of America's population (enrolled tribal members) are rapidly reversing the settling of the West, replacing state authority and protections with tribal jurisdictions, and expanding tribal land bases far beyond reservations. While tribes can purchase elected officials and block-vote their members in elections, Congress remains their Santa Claus and lowly Americans of any other ethnicity are indentured servants—in perpetuity.

I'm not aware of any living Native Americans who are not currently assimilated. I don't know an Indian that's never been in a vehicle, used a telephone, television, enjoyed McDonalds, put quarters in a slot machine, or received high-tech medical services. But hey, tribes want their Old Life Ways back, their "aboriginal" lands back. They want America's yesterday, today and tomorrow…and 574tribes are getting it done incrementally, and the process is accelerating every year.

Tribes are getting great support from environmentalists not fond of America and have major resources available through the Indigenous Peoples Movement and other policies of the United Nations.

While their governments fund America's politicians and orchestrate block votes in local, state and federal elections, tribes have overwhelmed Washington D.C. and dozens of state capitols as well. Note: we purchased their lands through treaties, and anything pre-constitutional or extra-constitutional is unconstitutional. If this is not true, America will soon be gone.

I don't really want my home on Stonybrook Drive in Anaheim back. But I surely don't want apartheid and purchased federal and state elected officials to take my country away either. Do you?

SECTION TWO

Corruption,
Here, There … Everywhere!

"We hang the petty thieves and elect the great ones to public office."

— Aesop

CHAPTER 7

An Open Letter to President Donald J. Trump

Honorable Donald J. Trump
President of the United States
White House
1600 Pennsylvania Avenue
Washington D.C., 20006

September 17, 2019

ASSERTION: Since its origins in the 1830's (judicial, legislative, administrative) all of federal Indian policy is: 1) entirely unconstitutional; 2) denies full American citizens enrolled in tribal governments their 14th Amendment protections and civil rights; 3) compels forced reparations *in perpetuity* upon American taxpayers to annually subsidize all basic needs and services of 573 tribal governments; and 4) permits tax-exempt tribal casinos and other tribal enterprises to undermine the marketplace of the tax-paying economy in thousands of communities across the nation.

Dear President Trump:

I have attached a brief professional statement supportive of the contents of this letter. Below is a cursory chronology that describes the increasing spread of tribalism as a governing system replacing our Republic form of government in America, and supports the assertion noted above.

1830   Chief Justice James Marshall issued three Indian-related rulings known as the Marshall Trilogy in 1830. With no support found in the U.S. Constitution, Marshall instead drew from international law to declare that the federal government had a "trust" relationship with its individual, dependent ward Indians. The Judiciary was the impetus for the origins of the federal trust relationship. In compliance with the Judiciary, Congress and the Executive Branch forged the Bureau of Indian Affairs and began the incremental expansion of tribalism as a governing system in the United States increasingly expanding for two centuries.

1871   The first half of the 1800s brought the formation of the Bureau of Indian Affairs, congressional statutes and administrative laws, managing Indian treaties, tribes, annual subsidies, and peacekeeping needs.

1887   Congress implemented efforts from the 1870s through 1924 to bring American Indians to full and equal citizenship with all other citizens, by ending the reservation system, tribal governments, and allowing Indians to be individual landowners and full citizens of their respective states.

1924   Congress passed the Snyder Act of 1924 making all American Indians full citizens.

1934 An avowed and self-proclaimed Communist, John Collier, became Commissioner of the Bureau of Indian Affairs, and persuaded Congress to pass the Indian Reorganization Act (IRA) of 1934. This created separate communal tribal governments and created dual citizenship that denies enrolled tribal members their 14th Amendment and Civil Rights. IRA has been an intentional and incremental deterrent for individual tribal civil rights and ownership of land.

1968 Congress passed the Indian Civil Rights Act (ICRA) to provide tribal members with civil rights but failed to provide any enforcement process for aggrieved tribal members. For over fifty years Congress has assumed that tribal members have civil rights under ICRA, but the reality is, lacking enforcement mechanism, tribal members have nothing.

1978 Congress passed the Indian Child Welfare Act (ICWA) transferring full parental authority from tribal parents to the tribal government. The benign intent was to preserve culture, but the reality for tribal families is that ICWA is often used as a weapon to punish or otherwise influence tribal families at risk of the tribal government taking their children — sometimes forever. The stated purpose and implementation of the ICWA is "the best interest of the tribe" and not "the best interest of a child." ICWA, drug addiction and suicides have been completely devastating to family units within Indian reservations.

1988 Congress passed the Indian Gaming Regulatory Act (IGRA) to provide tribes with economic self-sufficiency and ultimately offset and reduce annual federal subsidies. These tax-exempt gaming profits are *'free money'* to tribes, since federal subsidies continue to annually fund all basic services of 574 tribal governments. Casino funds are used to acquire land, hire legal counsel, hire lobbyists and fund candidate campaigns.

2000 Federal Election Commission Advisory Opinion (FEC-AO 2000-05) authorized tribal governments to financially and directly participate in funding political parties, incumbents or candidates. No other American governments may do so. But 574 tribal governments monetize America's elections while being exempt from most federal and state decisions made by legislators that tribes elect.

2012 Congress passed the HEARTH Act under the Obama administration, allowing tribal governments to long-term lease federal Indian 'trust' lands to middle eastern countries for up to 75 years, *without* BIA oversight or approval. Note that in 1904, Secretary of Interior A.B. Fall required all major dams, water and energy systems in Western states to be located on or near Indian reservation. The HEARTH Act affords opportunity for adversaries of this country close proximity to the nation's energy systems and power grids on lands receiving little or no state or local observation or oversight.

2014 Accelerating tribal involvement in the nation's power grid, Congress passed the Indian Energy Policy Act authorizing multi-billions of dollars for tribal governments to acquire major power infrastructure by a government that: 1) has no duty to the customer base, and 2) is protected by "sovereign immunity" from liability to the American people.

The original 1830 'trust' relationship was intended to be with individual Indians, but for perhaps expediency, Congress and federal agencies worked exclusively with tribal governments, unfortunately to the detriment of the tribal members they serve. Nationally, this massive issue impacting America is a *best kept secret* as most federal, state and local decisions are made in private communications with elected officials, administrators and tribal leaders. Minimal to no public hearing or input from tribal members and the general public occurs. Yet the enormity of the annual financial burden upon taxpayers and increasing loss of lands within states no longer served by a republic form of government quietly expands, year after year.

All of this can be viewed as forced reparations *in perpetuity* that saddles innocent American tax payers annually with the sins of yesterday, long since and abundantly compensated for over two centuries by such unconstitutional largesse — going to governments never contemplated in our country's Constitution.

I remain so deeply grateful for your election as our President in 2016, and eagerly look forward to your reelection in 2020. In your second term, my belief is that you alone can persuade your colleagues in the Executive Branch and members of Congress to restore the United States to One Nation Under God, and make the following requests:

1. To Make and Keep America Great, end the spread of tribalism as an unconstitutional governing system in the United States by restoring the United States of America to *"One nation under God"*;

2. End federal Indian policy and the existence of 574 'quasi-sovereign', separate nations within the United States;

3. Rescind FEC Advisory Opinion 2000-05, eliminating any tribal government funding of elections and candidates (***this action should be taken immediately, prior to the 2020 election***);

4. Restore full citizenship to enrolled tribal members, including their civil rights and the 14th Amendment;

5. Return all land held in title by the United States in "trust" for tribal governments to tribes, and transfer jurisdiction of such land to the respective states;

6. And establish a reasonable time certain by which all tribal governments and Indian reservations are terminated.

Very Sincerely Yours,

Elaine D. Willman
Ronan, Montana

Courage is what it takes to stand up and speak;
courage is also what it takes to sit down and listen.

—Winston Churchill

CHAPTER 8

The American Colonists and Montana Citizens — *Déja Vu* in 2017

"If ever a time should come, when vain and aspiring men shall possess the highest seats in Government, our country will stand in need of its experienced patriots to prevent its ruin."

— Sam Adams, 1776

The Confederated Salish and Kootenai Tribes (CSKT) Water Compact approved in April 2015 is the Revolutionary War for citizens of Montana. Its consequences are as severe. Where American colonists had lost the ear and trust in their British leaders, so too have Montanans lost the ear and trust in their State elected officials. And the Compact is only the beginning. There will be more: Kerr Dam, the Columbia River Treaty, threats of the CSKT initializing "repatriation" of their entire reservation, forcing non-tribal members off of their properties and off of the reservation.

Does this sound over the top? It is not. A small tribe of some 5,000 members led by aggressive, hostile leadership emboldened by every available federal agency and resource is in full assault mode to remove state authority within the reservation boundary, and likely within 11 western counties. Without firing a shot heard around the world, the CSKT has found that slathering money, false guilt and smear campaigns are more effective weapons to coerce Montana elected officials into obedience to a tribal government for which they have no duty.

Governor Bullock, Attorney General Fox, both federal Senators Daines and Tester and apparently the majority of Montana's Legislature are ignoring two major U.S. Supreme Court rulings, along with the Montana State Constitution, and have intentionally turned their backs on Montana citizens. In *OHA v. Hawaii* (2009) the U.S. Supreme Court ruled that land may not be removed from a state's authority, jurisdiction or tax base without approval of the state legislature. In *Tarrant v. Herrmann* (2013) the Supreme Court unanimously ruled that States have "the absolute right and authority over all navigable waters and the soils beneath them for lands ceded to a State upon statehood." Has the State of Montana picked up these two judicial tools to defend Article IX of its Constitution, or the rights of Montana citizens? Nope.

Has the State of Montana spent multi-million dollars over more than a decade to accommodate every single whim of the small CSKT? Yep. The feeble explanation is "to avoid litigation" when litigation of an unconstitutional compact will be considerably less costly to taxpayers compared to billions paid to the CSKT in perpetuity. Does such accommodation of CSKT whims as ambiguously buried within 1,500 pages of garbage promise many more multi-billions of Montana tax dollars to the CSKT in perpetuity? Yep.

Within the 1,500 pages of the proposed Compact, is there a single benefit to the State of Montana, 11 counties or 350,000 residents? Absolutely nothing. The Compact is not a "negotiation." Absent any benefit to the State or its citizens, the proposed CSKT Compact is a full and complete Surrender Document. Has the State guaranteed the loss of state water jurisdiction, municipal and private water rights, the loss of State and Federal constitutional and civil rights of 350,000 Montana citizens? Sadly, yes. And what does the State gain? Nada. Nothing.

Much like the Revolutionary War started on a bridge in one of the 13 colonies, this 2014 Revolutionary War starting on the CSKT Reservation in Montana will spread quickly to other states. Tribes share their "best practices" and coercive strategies with other tribes. The federal government under the former administration long ago ceased to be a friend to States or citizens. Too many state legislators are blinded by shiny things like federal funds and political correctness, to adhere to their one sworn Oath to protect their state resources and citizens.

The willing Paul Reveres within 11 affected Montana counties, must get on their horse, loudly gallop and shout throughout the valleys and the Rockies — that the Feds are coming, the Tribes are coming, the end of the balance of power between the federal government and states is near. Publicly expose the Turncoats in Montana, beginning with Governor Bullock, Attorney General Tim Fox, Senators Daines and Tester and a team of treacherous legislators; you know exactly who they are.

State elected officials should have been the first line of defense. In Montana, this line has fallen, and it is now up to Montana citizens to require and quickly breathe new courage and life into Montana elected officials, or prepare to defend your properties one parcel at a time, as best you can. Montanans have more resources now (cars, busses, phones, internet) than our countrymen had in the Revolutionary War in the 1700s, so get this done!

Save your state, your country, your property, your water and your American liberties. Given the choice of mad or sad, choose mad. Sad paralyzes. Mad energizes. Constructive use of anger can save the day within the Montana Legislature and among Montana citizens. The rest of the country is praying and watching. Get up off the couch and on your horse! Ride for your life in Montana.

To argue with a person who has renounced the use of reason
is like administering medicine to the dead."
— Thomas Paine

CHAPTER 9

Indian Casinos... Too Big to Fail

I magine a major Indian casino, the Mohegan Sun in Connecticut, reporting that its slot revenues reported to the state in April have "stabilized," slipping only 1 percent.

The same casino reported $1.3 billion (with a "B") in gross revenue for 2009. However, the economy is still dark, customers have less disposable income to slough into the tax-exempt slots, and the casino, in 2010, was facing a $15 million lawsuit for a head-on wreck caused by a drunken customer.

So, every member of Connecticut's congressional officials (except for one on travel) wants to ensure that the Mohegan Sun does not fail; that its "job creation" is always protected. These fool elected officials promoted and then awarded Stimulus funding of $54 MILLION dollars) in the form of a guaranteed loan from USDA to this mega-wealthy tribe.

And if they default? No problem. Tribes have sovereign immunity. Taxpayers whose taxes are already annually subsidizing this and 574 other Indian tribes in 35 states for all basic needs—housing, health, law enforcement, roads, environment, scholarships, language, cultural preservation — YES, you and I, our children and grandchildren, will just continually pay off the casino debts in perpetuity across the country. Taxpayers get to:

1) Annually fund all basic needs of tribal governments:

2) Cover all tribal uncollectible debt due to "sovereign immunity;" and

3) Keep throwing dollars into tax-exempt tribal slot machines across the country so our local economies get sufficiently and systematically drained of tax revenues and tax-paying businesses that cannot compete.

To make this work, taxpayers must faithfully commit to frequenting tax-exempt tribal government businesses. But now it doesn't matter if you choose not. They're too big to fail; the federal agencies will step in and bill you for their losses, anyway.

There are 245 other tribes in the lower 48 states entitled to the same perks as the Mohegan Sun. Fortunately, the 228 tribes in Alaska who receive the basic-needs funding, at least don't have casinos yet. Alaskan tribes are non-profit corporations without jurisdictional authority or gaming so they focus almost entirely on their culture. What a concept!

First a few facts: 574 federally recognized (tax-exempt) tribes are located in 35 hosts states, of which 246 tribes are gaming under the Indian Gaming Regulatory Act of 1988. Every host state to numerous tribal tax-exempt and tax-eroding tribal governments and reservations are coincidentally the states experiencing the largest state budget deficits.

It is thus far impossible to calculate the annual cost of this race-based socialist system spreading across the country. Former Commerce Secretary Gary Locke reported $94 million in Stimulus Funding for the tribes in Washington State alone, back in 2010. We're hearing 4 billion annually just for tribal health care; many more billions for housing, law enforcement, etc. And these dollars do not include the "Tribal Priority Allocations" doled out annually by the Bureau of Indian Affairs. There are 29 federal agencies — each with a separate budget for funding the 574 tribes. And worse, state governments have no "trust" or fiduciary duties to Indian Tribes. however, states such as Washington, Oregon, Montana and others, have self-inflicted a *duty*, a *state trust relationship* with Indian tribes too, and have set up separate state budgets within their state agencies to supplement federal dollars going out to tribes. This federal/state tax double-dipping is Strike Two for taxpayers. All of these federal and state dollars are serving less than 1 million enrolled tribal members, less than one-half of 1% of our 350+ million American population.

Who can blame the Native Hawaiians for wanting in on this lucrative industry, forever chaining down American citizens to the galley oars of a feudal federal Indian policy system? Thankfully, the Akaka Bill (Native Hawaiian Government Reorganization Act) has continually failed in Congress or these numbers could considerably worsen.

Since the Indian Reorganization Act of 1934 federal Indian policy has been an 8-decades private conversation between federal agencies, elected officials and tribal leaders, with the whopping bills deducted from your federal and state tax contributions annually. We simply can no longer afford to sustain and grow this socialist erosion spreading across 35 and perhaps 36 (Hawaii) states.

One of our astute Supreme Court Justices assessed our predicament accurately when he noted the following, over 20 years ago:

"Individuals who have been wronged by unlawful racial discrimination should be made whole; but under our Constitution there can be no such thing as either a creditor or a debtor race. That concept is alien to the Constitution's focus upon the individual. ... To pursue the concept of racial entitlement — even for the most admirable and benign of purposes — is to reinforce and preserve for future mischief the way of thinking that produced race slavery, race privilege and race hatred. In the eyes of government, we are just one race here. It is American."

— Justice Antonin Scalia,
Adarand Constructors, Inc. v. Mineta, 534 U.S. 103 (1995)

Here is the problem: Over forty years ago, in 1975 Congress passed the Indian Self-Determination and Education (IDEA) Act to promote economic self-sufficiency for tribal governments. Apparently this was not working well enough, so nearly thirty years ago, Congress added the economic steroid of a tax-free gaming monopoly for Indian tribes when it passed the Indian Gaming Regulatory Act in 1988.

In March of 2010, George Skibine, an Assistant Secretary at the Bureau of Indian Affairs (BIA) was a keynote speaker at Washington, D.C. conference. Mr. Skibine was asked: "Has the Department of Interior (DOI) or Bureau of Indian Affairs ever developed criteria or measuring systems by which a tribal government might be deemed economically self-sufficient, and no longer in need of federal funds?" The answer was no. Not in forty years so far. Not even with a gaming monopoly. The follow-up question: "Does the DOI/BIA have any *interest* in establishing such economic indicators so that federal subsidies could be redirected to either write down our national deficit, or redirected to the poorest tribes?" The answer was no again. Why should they? The behemoth BIA bureaucracy staff grows exponentially as the number and needs of tribal governments grow.

Also, at the D.C. conference Mr. Skibine was asked if the BIA or federal government could ascertain the total annual federal funds expended for tribal governments. His response: "We tried to do that once, but were unable to." Astounding! No one knows the annual bottomless pit of taxpayer dollars supporting tribal governments.

So there you have it. We are enslaved forever by our Congressmen to a burgeoning number of private tax-exempt, race-based governments that we are forced to fund unknown annual billions in perpetuity. And now we must assume the responsibility for all failed tribal government debts. What can you do? Try any or all these suggestions:

1) Howl at every talking head on radio and television.

2) Get firm commitments from incumbents or candidates to put a "sunset" or end game in place for this tax-enslavement.

3) Get federal legislation that prohibits gaming tribes from receiving taxpayer bailouts of any sort for failing tribal businesses.

4) Get legislation in place that ends any further "federal recognition" of future wannabe tribes. (A GAO Report of 2014 lists 400 future tribes waiting to be federally recognized!)

We were stuck with the former administration throwing more huge tax dollars out to tribes. We were stuck with the government takeover of multiple industries in this country under the former administration.

The current federal administration has not exacerbated the expansion of federally funded tribal policies but has done little to rein in or reduce this burden on the shoulders of Americans.

We are *not* stuck with our elected officials. We have been getting a few responsible commitments from federal and state elected officials since 2016. We must build support for ending this race-based perpetual burden on Americans, and get spineless elected officials out office,

We are only as helpless and indentured, as we are silent.

And we best get busy. Tribal governments claim to plan for seven generations. That is a long time for Americans to be indentured servants to one ethnicity. Ada Deer, a leader of the American Indian Movement (AIM), a Menominee Tribal leader and former BIA Director under Bruce Babbitt and the Clinton administration, once said, "We use the system to beat the system." They certainly do. It is time to end this race-based abuse of the "system" and American taxpayers.

A body of men holding themselves accountable to nobody
ought not to be trusted by anybody"

— Thomas Paine

CHAPTER 10

Federal Takeover
of State Sovereign Authority...

Property Rights and Citizen Civil Rights, to Achieve Removal
of Crop Production in Western States

H ere is the Big Picture of a collection of federal programs cramming down right now on individual landowners in Western States, and specifically, Western Montana:

1. All **Western Watershed Management Plans** for the great rivers (Missouri, Mississippi, Columbia, etc.) have transitioned their primary purpose from agriculture and economic development to "tribal sovereign cultural resources, ESA, etc.). Irrigation is now at the bottom of the list for use of major river waters.

2. **Capturing state waters** using tribal governments as pawns. (See CSKT Compact, Klamath Dams, etc.).

3. **BIA-owned/controlled power and energy entities.** Now requires ALL customers of **BIA-owned/controlled power or energy** entities to provide extensive and intrusive personal information (i.e. social security numbers, EIN numbers, # of acres owned, annual water/ power use, number of persons in households, household incomes, etc. (See March 31, 2016 Federal Register).

4. **Indian Energy Program** as "Indian Economic development" to transfer public utilities (dams, energy plants) from public utilities to tribal sovereign assets. (Billions of dollars and huge federal facilitation for tribes to take over major pockets of our nation's power grid.

5. Obama's federal **"Drought Resilience" Program**, with complete capability of pinning down individual landowners. (See Federal Register, Presidential Proclamation, March 21, 2016).

6. The **CSKT Compact** on the Flathead Reservation and directly impacting 11 Western Montana counties. Approved by Montana Legislature, April 11, 2015.

7. **Transfer of Kerr Dam to CSKT**, September 5, 2015. Now all water rates (wholesale and retail) are controlled and collected by the feds/ tribe with NO caps, and NO review by Montana Public Services Commission.

8. **Mission Valley Power Company**. Owned by BIA, operated by CSKT. Now wholesale and retail electric rates have NO caps, and NO review by Montana Public Services Commission.

It would be impossible for our friends and neighbor landowners here on the Flathead Indian Reservation to be completely aware of all of these forces and processes bearing directly down on their own individual lands, intended to take out crop production here and across the Western States. The ultimate goal is to take out landowners, property rights, and replace State authority with federal/tribal jurisdiction in wide swaths. But it IS happening right NOW, and has been quietly developed by multiple agencies for a couple of decades. **Failure of landowners to act makes it a certainty. In Western Montana, crop production IS our economy.**

And NO government will help. All governments are intentionally adversarial to the landowner. We ONLY have the federal court.

The GOOD News: All of the above constitutes a whole volume of federal violations of the U.S. Constitution, Montana State Constitution, Tribal Constitution, egregious violations of the federal Administrative Procedures Act (APA) such as due process, discrimination, — actually this whole collusion of federal agencies constitutes a Racketeering (RICO) violation, violates the Sherman Antitrust Act, which applies to the Federal Government, and countless other laws and regulations.

The irony is that the black/white printed law is on OUR side since all these agencies have intentionally gone rogue and no longer follow their own regulations or any laws. Court is our only hope, but court will be clumsy and tedious at first, moving through the lower courts (most filled with Obama appointees), then up to the Appellate Court where help should come (even from the unpredictable 9th Circuit).and on up to the Supreme Court.

Americans are so enamored of equality,
they would rather be equal in slavery than unequal in freedom.

— Alex De Toqueville

CHAPTER 11

The U.S. Census Bureau = Duplicity, Duplication and Racism

"The actual Enumeration shall be made within three Years after the first Meeting of the Congress of the United States, and within every subsequent Term of ten Years, in such Manner as they shall by Law direct. The number of Representatives shall not exceed one for every thirty Thousand, but each State shall have at Least one Representative;" [Article I, Section 2]

How do you grow a federal agency that has one Constitutional task to accomplish every ten years? Get very racially creative. Since the 14th Amendment was ratified on July 9, 1868 any racial disparity of the original Constitution was repealed.

The formal 2010 U.S. Census short form this year contains 10 simple questions that can be answered in approximately 10 minutes. The short form is the *only* Constitutional mandate of the U.S. Census bureau and is mailed to every known address in the United States. Who knows these addresses? The U.S. Post Office and most bulk mailers. Does the U.S. Census bureau coordinate their needs with their federal counterpart, the U.S. Post Office? No. They start at ground zero with the formation of the Local Update of Census Addresses (LUCA) Program which requires hundreds of thousands of staff working through all 12 regional offices of the U.S. Census Bureau. The cost to taxpayers for the Census Bureau's failure to avail itself of known address information is in the billions. But the cost is now measured in more than mere dollars.

Who else knows data needed by the U.S. Census Bureau? Our federal Social Security Agency which has tracked all citizens having social security cards (some, shortly after birth) since at least 1935 under Roosevelt's New Deal. Does the Census Bureau avail itself of social security data? No. Again, it hires inordinate staff in 12 regional offices to develop from ground zero, data that has been long-time available from other federal agencies. Silo thinking among federal agencies facilitates federal agency expansions, job security and bloating costs further burdening taxpayers.

Granted, the Constitutional data requirements guide the Census Bureau in the formation of congressional districts and federal funding in the billions, by state, county and municipalities. Yet the Census Bureau disregards data collection based upon boundaries of some existing 3,141 counties or nearly 40,000 incorporated municipalities. The Bureau, in contrast, sets up its own "boundaries" with land tracts, blocks and groups for purpose of data collection. This is a curious redundancy when the ultimate population results must also be transposed back into populations of these existing counties and municipalities.

The data is essential to even-handed representation and funding. The **un**even-handed Census Bureau outcomes are achieved during the nine years when the Census Bureau is not accomplishing its one primary task. A good example is the *American Community Survey* (ACS) that is not a Constitutional mandate.

The ACS is administered through the Chicago Regional Office that hires "federal employees" across the country to develop, administer, distribute and collect data from the ACS, a task that keeps Census Bureau employees gainfully employed for at least seven of the years of downtime in between a ten-year task. Assume three years of activity gearing up for, during and after a Decennial Census, then look at all the racial data collected that becomes special preference programs for a plethora of ethnicities, when the Constitutional mandate is so simple: Count every American citizen once every ten years.

On its website, the Census Bureau reports, "The full implementation of the ACS began with 2005 data collection — expanding the survey coverage from 1,239 counties to all of the nation's 3,141 counties, as well as Puerto Rico, American Indian reservations, Alaska native villages and Hawaiian Home Lands. The opportunity for overcounting is significant here.

Does or should the Census Bureau coordinate its data needs with the federal Immigration and Naturalization Service (INS)? It could coordinate its data with yet another federal counterpart, but there is no ethnic requirement of the Decennial Census. It is interesting that expansion of racial classification through the ACS came under the Obama Administration which aggressively promoted "Diversity" the division of Americans by skin color and ethnicity.

Here is just one example of overlap and duplication: Every single one of Indian reservations (current or former) in the lower 48 States is co-located within a county and/or municipality. These Indian Reservations are predominantly non-Indian in population (Navajo and Red Lake reservations being rare exceptions). Tribal members are full U.S. citizens residing within a county…period.

Where the ethnic creativity of the U.S. Census Bureau ran off the rails was a bright idea fostered by the National Congress of American Indians in 2004. They passed a resolution demanding direct involvement in Census Bureau activities to better count their members. Of course, every single tribal government maintains a precise list of its enrolled tribal members but does not share that confidential information with federal or state agencies. Tribes know exactly who is enrolled, who lives on, or who lives off of their reservations. Tribal members are actually counted twice: once among enrolled lists of tribal governments, and once as residents of the county in which they reside. So a national tribal organization whose tribal government members already know their exact respective populations chastised and shamed the Census Bureau for undercounting tribal members, while continuously refusing to share their records.

The response to the National Congress of American Indians was egregious and unconstitutional. The Local Update of Census Addresses (LUCA) Program changed its game. In June 2007 former Director of the U.S. Census Bureau, Charles Kincannon sent letters out to 1,061 representative governments (cities, towns, counties) informing these local governments that since their government was located on or within an Indian reservation, for purpose of the 2010 Census, their governments were "not relevant;" that the "relevant government" was the tribal government.

Yes, tribal governments with no duty to citizens who are not enrolled tribal members would be conducting the tasks formative for the 2010 Census on their current, diminished or former reservations that are predominantly non-Indian. And, tribal governments could choose to share collected census data with neighboring governments, or not. Fortunately, numerous complaints to the Secretary of Commerce and his Legal Counsel, quickly caused a "legal review" of the LUCA program, and by December 2008, all 1,061 representative governments received a second letter from Mr. Kincannon. He advised them that they were in fact, "relevant" for the Decennial Census, and that the Census Bureau would restore its LUCA program to the policies of the 2000 Census. Mr. Kincannon retired shortly thereafter.

Before getting this secret tribal-focused LUCA program stopped, however, between 2004 and late 2007 census workers sent teams out to countless tribal governments to train tribal members in census tasks, at an incalculable cost to taxpayers but great job expansion and security to the Census Bureau, and marvelous travel experiences too.

Unfortunately, the LUCA program's actual implementation policies have not been fully restored. In May 2008, local "relevant" governments located within or near Indian reservations updated and supplied their address information to the Census Bureau. Then in May 2009 the Chicago regional office of the Census Bureau hired only tribal members to "verify" addresses on "Indian reservations." When a sufficient number of tribal members to be hired as census workers could not be found, non-Indian workers were hired.

Hiring non-Indian census workers drew immediate outrage from the Chicago office. Non-Indian workers were terminated and told to "get off the reservation." Millions of American citizens who are not tribal members live within the boundaries of Indian reservations. The Census Bureau continues to hijack the census from the responsibility of local representative governments to employ only tribal members. This is racial discrimination to the extreme because tribal governments strongly influence their members, and tribal governments have no incentive whatsoever to ensure an accurate count of households or populations of representative (town, city county) governments co-located within an Indian reservation

Racializing the data, the policies, the workers and key leadership of the U.S. Census foments special preference federal funding based upon ethnicity alone, whether it is for American Indians, Hispanics, Blacks or any other ethnicity. The U.S. Census Bureau has taken a simple task, that of counting every American citizen once, to a higher priority of breaking down American society into racial categories and pitting one race against another for federal program funding. How this affects congressional representation can be calculated by ethnic related lobbyists and special interest groups, and their influence upon elected officials.

I am Cherokee and deeply proud of the history and strength of my ancestry. But I am first, an American citizen that should be counted one time only, by the government that represents me, my municipality and county. At no time should a private (tribal) government be involved with the Decennial Census upon which I, and all Americans, rely. Because I live within a former Indian reservation but am not an enrolled member of that tribe, I cannot even participate in the Decennial Census handed over to a government that would prefer I lived elsewhere.

Once upon a time, from 1868 until 2005, there was certainty that the primary purpose of the U.S. Census was an accurate count of America's population. Today, we endure a bloated federal agency with a clear racial agenda to segment American society and federal funding by ethnicity…all for political influence and job security of a federal agency with one thing to do…every ten years. These behind-the-scene policies promote increasing race-polarization and policy decisions made by our elected officials of all political affiliations. It's the race-based thumb on the scale that is erasing the opportunity for actual equality among American people.

It would seem as if the rulers of our time sought only to use men in order to make things great; I wish that they would try a little more to make great men; that they would set less value on the work and more upon the workman; that they would never forget that a nation cannot long remain strong when every man belonging to it is individually weak; and that no form or combination of social polity has yet been devised to make an energetic people out of a community of pusillanimous and enfeebled citizens

— Alex De Toqueville.

CHAPTER 12

My Country 'Tis of Tyranny...?

Four Socialist Horsemen of our Apocalypse

There are four forces that have been moving across our country for decades, on separate but parallel paths, and are in full assault today. All four threaten individual liberty, property rights, and the relationship between the citizen, our states and the federal government: 1) massive illegal immigration; 2) rapid expansions of federal Indian policy; 3) a verifiable Deep State transitioning a republic form of government to a centralized and socialized system of government.; and 4) Globalists pushing forward with the One World Order.

Two of the above forces (immigration and globalism) are external pressures on our country, and two are internal (Indian policy and the Deep State). What do these forces have in common? Socialism, the fluffy word for communism. Socialism comes through persuasion, opening the door to communism, by force.

A military term, *Pincer Movement*, is defined by Merriam-Webster dictionary as: an attack by two coordinated forces that close in on an enemy position from different directions. We have four "coordinated forces" taking down our Constitutional protections and form of government.

Any one of these movements is deeply concerning, but the cumulative impact in 2020 and moving forward is the tyranny taking down the Founding principles of the U.S. Constitution...the voice and guaranteed protections of We The People.

Federal Indian Policy

This discussion focuses on the impact of federal Indian policy as it affects the balance of power between the federal government and the states. However, this discussion needs to be viewed with the awareness of at least three other forces simultaneously tearing at the fabric of our country's governing system:

> *"Imagine a country that has a corrupt authoritarian government. In that country no one knows about checks and balances or an independent court system. Private property is not recognized in that country either. Neither can one buy or sell land. And businesses are reluctant to bring investments into this country. Those who have jobs usually work for the public sector. Those who don't have jobs subsist on entitlements that provide basic food. At the same time, this country sports a*

free health care system and free access to education. Can you guess what country it is? It could be the former Soviet Union, Cuba, or any other socialist country of the past. Yet, I want to assure you that such a country exists right here in the United States...And its name is Indian Country." — Native American Reservations: *"Socialist Archipelagos,"* by Andrei Znamenski

As stated in Professor Znamenski's illuminating article, the reservation system serves 22% of some 5 million Indians, and polka-dots thirty-eight states in America, but less than 1% of America's population. Currently 574 tribes are federally recognized in this scheme that entirely disrupts the balance of power between the federal government and the states.

For decades the Department of Justice and Department of Interior have been using the "plenary" authority of Congress, combined with federal War Powers to create and utilize "Federal Reserve Rights" over land and water. The War Powers Act is never to be used against states but has been the underlying force exercised in federal Indian policy by the Department of Interior since at least the mid-1850s.

Federal Indian policy is decision-making enacted by Congress, federal agencies, and states. Tribal governments are not the source; they are the recipients. Tribes are recipients as the sole ethnicity that owns the American Eagle and its feathers, for example, unavailable to other Americans. In the Northwest tribes control another species, the Salmon, diminishing the availability of salmon to non-tribal sources. Working with the U.S. Fish and Wildlife, tribes are claiming certain plants within national forests as their indigenous foods, to be restrained from non-tribal forest visitors. Apparently, there's no Hispanic or Settlers foods of any consequence. Using this mentality, tribes can soon claim that timber and wood sustains their cultural as well, and there goes the national forests completely, pushed through the legislative and legal system.

The Facilitators of Indian Socialism

Two key sources are facilitating the expansion of tribal control over state lands, waters and resources:

1. Timid, coin-operated elected officials at every level of government; and

2. A massive, profiteering legal industry incessantly working to revise and reverse America's history with Indians, all of whom are full citizens with full rights under the Constitution.

Elected officials are timid because should they dare to deny tribal government demands, they are immediately labeled as racist, shamed or intentionally run out of office by tribal government funding of opponents and tribal government block voting. An example of this would be former Washington State Senator Slade Gorton, replaced by Senator Maria Cantwell when Senator Gorton had the nerve to suggest that federal funding be reduced and redirected from wealthy gaming tribes to poorer non-gaming tribes (*means testing*).

Another example would be Montana's Senator Jon Tester, who caters to all things tribal, ignoring his Oath and duty to other Montanans because he can count on massive tribal election funding, and election shenanigans. On numerous Indian reservations block voting occurs, and many polling precincts are exempt from **any** State oversight. Stuffing ballot boxes and individually purchased votes on Indian reservations put Tester in office in 2006 and has kept him in office ever since.

The Federal Election Commission in Advisory Opinion of 2000-05 determined that tribal governments may directly, financially contribute to political parties, incumbents or candidates. No other American governments may do so.

Conflict is marketing power for attorneys and the stuff of litigation. As tribal governments reach back to reverse history, law firms across the country are only too happy to help. Though taxpayers fund these socialist tribal governments to the tune of billions of dollars annually, the same tribal governments seem to have limited resources with which to upgrade the quality of life among their people on reservations, yet there seems to be no limit on tribal funding availability for lawyers to go after the United States.

Attorneys prosper and love this stuff and wealthy tribes are more than happy to push America back to "pre-colonizing" days. Tribes are magnificently succeeding in biting the hand that feeds them, with the full cooperation of the *hands* — legislators, lawyers and the federal government.

The Constitutional Disruption of Socialism

How is all of this disrupting the Constitutional balance of power between the federal government and states? The Constitution never contemplated separate, quasi-sovereign nations within land ceded to a state. The Constitution prohibits War powers against a state. States hosting Indian tribes have no "Equal footing" with states that have no Indian reservations. Today, several states have governors, attorneys general and legislators who make decisions that elevate tribal "sovereignty" as superior to its own Constitutional state sovereignty. Money talks. Attorneys will argue anything for a dime. Liberal judges will play ball with their colleague legal industry. *What* Constitution? That outdated old rag?

Thanks to our legislators and litigators tribal government authority is penetrating national parks, national monuments, national forests, and incrementally removing state taxable lands from lands ceded to the respective states and transferring them into tax-exempt federal lands. The sovereignty and jurisdictional authority of states are in severe trouble. All of America is as well, beginning with the total erosion of our Constitution.

Attempts at Restoring the Constitution

Several states are finally turning to the U.S. Supreme Court arena to protect what's left of their state sovereignty:

➤ **Washington.** The Washington Culvert case is based upon a collection of tribes asserting tribal sovereignty over Washington lands and waters (culverts) as superior to State sovereignty (*Washington State v. United States*, 584 U.S. (2018).

➤ **Wyoming** is currently defending its state sovereign authority from a Montana tribe, the Crow that is claiming its members have treaty rights in Wyoming; rights that were long ago abandoned with Wyoming's statehood (*Herrera v. Wyoming*, USSC 17-532).

➤ **New Jersey** prevailed in a recent ruling of the U.S. Supreme Court (*Murphy v. NCAA*, No. 16-476) reasserting the "anti-commandeering" doctrine: "As the Tenth Amendment confirms, all legislative power not conferred on Congress by the Constitution is reserved for the States. Absent from the list of conferred powers is the power to issue direct orders to the governments of the States...Congress may not simply 'commandeer the legislative process of the States by directly compelling them to enact and enforce a federal regulatory program.'"

➤ **Oklahoma** is defending its statehood that ended the reservation system in Oklahoma from tribes claiming its reservation boundaries never went away (USSC *Carpenter v. Murphy*, citation pending).

This Oklahoma case, should Oklahoma be defeated, will resurrect half of the state's lands to replace state jurisdiction with that of the five Civilized tribes.

➤ **Wisconsin.** A Wisconsin tribe is claiming that their reservation fully allotted and disestablished in 1892, never happened. The Oneida tribe now claims in 2020 that their former reservation is *Indian Country* and should govern the counties and towns within it. (*Oneida Tribe of Indians of Wisconsin v. Village of Hobart*, US Fed. Distr. 16-C-1217). (Note: In this case, the tribe hired six highly paid national legal counsel to take on one municipal attorney). A ruling is pending.

Conclusion

There is hope on perhaps the not-so-distant horizon. In the very recent years, the U.S. Supreme Court has started taking a hard look and reining in federal government over-reach, working diligently to restore the infrastructure of our government to comport with the framework and intent of the Constitution. The Supreme Court is now questioning the federal governments use of war powers and asking federal attorneys to locate the plenary (omnipotent) power of Congress within the text of the Constitution. It isn't there. It is these two tools, plenary authority and war powers, that are the linchpins of federal Indian policy.

The incremental expansion of tribal jurisdiction and authority over state lands, waters and eco-systems, facilitated by federal statutes, regulations and regulatory agencies, is akin to federal *commandeering* states to blindly accept tribal sovereign authority as preferential, if not outright superior to the Constitutional sovereignty of the respective States.

While the four *Pincer* forces described herein are spreading socialism across our lands and infiltrating our government, the least known of these is federal Indian policy. It's a best kept secret between elected officials and tribal governments. Sometimes, the least known, most secretive and least addressed assault is the most successful.

Action is needed. More information, more public education and more vocal citizens would elevate the conversation on federal Indian policy to the levels now occurring with illegal immigration, the Deep State and the One World Order.

Standing in the middle of the road is very dangerous;
you get knocked down by traffic in both directions.
— Margaret Thatcher

CHAPTER 13

Flaming Forests and Cars

It is interesting to look at our crisis reactions. Some folks grab the video when someone's trapped in a burning car. Others are paralyzed in place by the frightening visual. And then there are those who leap for the car doors, break the windows and risk life to safe life.

Regarding burning cars, I'm not physically gifted and would likely stand in paralysis, perhaps screaming, and likely hitting 911 as fast as I could. But when it comes to the growing fears I have about what is happening in my country, I am ripping the car doors and breaking the windows to do all I can for my countrymen.

Americans, true citizens of the United States whose government serves them, are an openly endangered species, under assault. Landowners, growers and grazers have absolute targets on their back. The most aggressive predator was Obama's federal government by way of dozens of federal agencies answerable to the Executive Branch that were fully militarized and had boastfully gone rogue. EPA, USDA, USFW, BLM, and the other alphabet adversaries were whipping out new regulations that far exceed their authority or any intent of Congressional Acts and federal statutes. They were playing catch-me-if-you-can, trampling one landowner and one citizen after another. In 2020 the current Executive branch has not increased abhorrent regulations but has not rescinded over-reaching existing regulations so It is getting uglier by the day.

In Montana and other Western states it is more than one person trapped in a burning car. It is worse than the dozen flaming cars on the I-15 freeway at Cajon Pass in Southern California on July 17, 2015. It is equivalent to the entire length of the I-15 freeway full of families trapped in flaming cars from a federally started forest fire that jumped and captured the vehicles.

Why am I talking about fires? Fires can be viewed as Acts of God (clean hands) while federal mismanagement actually lights the fuse. Droughts can be viewed as Acts of Nature (clean hands) when intentional redirection and mismanagement of waters dries up wide swaths of productive land. Decades of federally mismanaged forests are escalating the ability for wildfires to destroy homes, properties, livelihoods. It's a tool of bureaucratic incrementalism, taking several hundred, maybe thousands of homes each year. Why the analogy of fires? They quickly go out of control, escalate and destroy unsuspecting citizen lives. Federal mis-managers walk away blameless.

Similarly, the USFW and EPA utilize the Endangered Species Act to denigrate real people, citizens in the United States to lesser importance than the snail darter, while holding the human accountable for destroying Planet Earth. Another tool of bureaucratic is the Boiling Frog incrementalism eroding property rights, citizen rights, and swallowing up in an escalating manner, otherwise productive (America's food) lands by thousands of acres each year.

Has anyone snapped to the newest maneuver to federally require extended "expiration dates" on consumer foods? That will at least temporarily salve federal agency activities that are intentionally diminishing America's food supply in the Northwest and Midwest. Just ask the growers and grazers in eleven western Montana Counties whose water has been confiscated, reduced, redirected or entirely lost to an egregious federal water compact by a triumvirate of federal, state and tribal governments.

The long-term implementation of the Confederated Salish-Kootenai Tribes (CSKT) Water Compact will entirely remove an irrigation system on the Flathead Indian Reservation that is the heart and soul of the economy of three counties within the Flathead Indian Reservation. Of course, that depopulates a reservation that is 90% non-Indian of the farmers and growers that have helped the Salish-Kootenai tribes on the Flathead Indian Reservation thrive for over 100 years.

Below is the recorded reality of the perils endured by the Salish-Kootenai tribes in the 1840s through the late 1800s as reported by their elder historians in a 1923 publication recently republished by the Salish Kootenai College. Revisionist history had not started in 1923; that came later in the 1970s and flamed up huge after the 1988 Indian Gaming Regulatory Act. The Salish-Kootenai tribes were getting fiercely and frequently attacked by Plains Indians competing for the bison hunts, losing dozens of their tribal members, and unable to hunt bison that provided the Salish-Kootenai's sole source of economy of the tribes at the time:

> "...tribal social organization and physical survival were threatened by the loss of people and property in the battles with the plains tribes. The rapidly expanding white population in western Montana competed with the Salish and Pend d'Oreille for land and resources, but also provided allies in

the war with the plains tribes…Some of the white invaders were useful military allies in the common war with the plains Indian tribes, and others provided war supplies — guns and ammunition and general trade goods. Still others brought new spiritual powers to protect the tribe…Most of the traditional economic activities continued, but the tribal economies were expanded by new sources of support introduced by the whites. Cattle ranching and farming broadened the tribal economic base and buffered the tribes when hunts were poor."

Challenge to Survive: History of the Salish Tribes
of the Flathead Indian Reservation
reproduced publication of 1923 report,
published by Salish Kootenai College, publication date not noted.

You're welcome. So, the response to the protections, support and economic expansions provided to the tribe by white settlers is to totally run their descendants off the land. Yes, you are welcome. Will you also run off electricity, automobiles, slot machines, flat screen TVs, cell phones and other accoutrements of the white settlers? Likely not.

The peril facing non-tribal landowners whose ancestors believed Congress and settled the West, including Indian reservations, is not coming from an Act of God or Nature. **Reversing** history and constant shaming of America is the lightning that started the fires of incendiary government decisions continuously coddling one ethnicity of Americans, while burdening all taxpayers with the cost, and driving off the families that built this great country.

There is nothing fair or productive for Americans, tribal or non-tribal, to continue this hoax.

Politics I suppose to be the second oldest profession. I have come to realize that it bears a very close resemblance to the first.

— Ronald Reagan

CHAPTER 14

Are Our Elected Officials Betraying Us?

L et's get one thing clear: Tribal governments do not create Federal Indian Policy. The Executive Branch, Congress and the Courts do. Tribal government officials, lobbyists and legal counsels of 574 tribes have been heavily persuasive with our elected officials at every level of government, but tribes do not make federal/state law.

The people you and I elect to every level of office make abundant decisions to benefit Indian tribes, generally to the direct harm of the state citizens served. As example, there were approximately 270 bills in Congress in 2017 alone, to benefit tribal governments.

Washington State is the *Poster Child* for having the most elected officials who have sworn an Oath to protect their State, its natural resources and citizens, but have continuously diverted their allegiance to the 29 tribes hosted by the State. From former Governor Mike Lowry to current Governor Jay Inslee, the State of Washington has been either unable or unwilling to preserve its State authority as superior to tribal sovereignty.

No state has a duty or "trust" relationship with Indian tribes unless a state willingly self-imposes such a condition. Only the federal government has a "trust" relationship. Governor Lowry, however, self-imposed a "trust" relationship between the State of Washington and its Indian tribes with the *Centennial Accord of 1989*. Government-to-government relations with tribes can be managed in the same manner as Washington conducts its relations with Oregon and Idaho — no fiscal or trust relationship with their neighboring states. There should be no state "trust" relationship with 29 Indian tribes either. The devastating economic harm is incalculable from the loss of control of state waters, air, natural resources, incrementally expanding for 29 tribes. Washington cannot grow its boundaries nor acquire new resources. But 29 sub-governments are internally confiscating state resources and lands incrementally at an escalating, overwhelming pace. As example, the Swinomish tribe was particularly aggressive while their Chairman Cladoosby was Chair of the National Congress of American Indians (NCAI), and the aggression continues today.

Of course, it's all about the money and political power of the tribes, but Washington voters are fully culpable for allowing these "coin-operated" elected officials to remain in office. The end result is that the state's elected officials cater to 2% of Washington's population (enrolled tribal members) to the immediate and permanent harm of 98% of Washington's population.

Washington's Senators Murray and Cantwell have a despicable voting pattern of supporting all federal and tribal efforts or whims to the direct harm of the state citizens that elected them. The Governor, Senators and Congressmen are not the only betrayers of their constitutions. With the exception of Skagit County officials, state Legislators, County Commissioners, City Council members seem to have a couple of problems: 1) they have either long forgotten their Oath to uphold federal and state constitutions; or 2) they are outright terrified of being called a name...like "racist."

A third problem for Washington's elected officials is the money and political power of tribes during elections. Tribal governments are the only governments in America that may cut checks directly to any/all political parties, PACS, incumbents or candidates. No other American governments may financially participate in local, state and federal elections.

The Voting Rights Act, which rightfully improved access to polls for individual Native Americans, never contemplated that tribal governments could orchestrate and force group/block voting of their enrolled members.

Remember former Senator Slade Gorton? Senator Gorton made the fatal suggestion that wealthy gaming tribes have their annual federal subsidies somewhat reduced and redirected to poor non-gaming tribes. That was sufficient to cause the Indian industry in Washington State to money up Senator Maria Cantwell in a very close election that brought bare victory to Cantwell when delayed ballots from Indian tribes gave her the lead. Washington lost a true statesman then, and similar shenanigans defeated Dino Rossi and others.

Here's the irony: the problem is you, the reader, you the voter in Washington State. Somehow insufficient support for elected officials who are life-sworn to protect their state and country has handed over Washington to 29 tribes. Citizens can change this starting today. Get front and center with current elected officials and demand they protect your constitutional, civil and property rights before any further expansion of tribal sovereignty in Washington. Then financially support such oath-keeping candidates or elected officials to counter tribally funded opponents.

We have all heard and endured ongoing *revisionist history,* but what has happened under previous Administrations and Congress is actually *reversing* history...intentionally unsettling the West.

Two things were going on in the 1800s: 1) Congress was truly working toward American Indians becoming full citizens, even landowners; and 2) Congress was settling the West.

The federal government purchased "ceded" lands from tribes and formed bounded reservation areas within which tribal communities could live any way they chose with the goal of full citizenship within two generations. Land and water within the reservation boundaries were owned by the United States, and the BIA had the sole governance, or jurisdictional enforcement capability. Tribal governments under treaties had no ownership, governance or jurisdiction over reservation lands or waters. Tribes had only federally protected *beneficial use and occupancy* of lands and waters...nothing more.

Throughout the 1800s Congress was yelling "Go West Young Man..." even on to homesteading Indian reservations. Young Man settled the West, created the ranches, farms, schools, churches, towns...and now Seattle, Spokane, Bellingham, Olympia, Yakima, etc. Young Man was given absolutely nothing from the federal government to do these great things. Indian tribes were given annual dollars, blacksmiths, food, housing, schools, doctors and other supplies. During this period of time until the end of the Civil War, Black Americans were sold like cattle. The *only* population continuously receiving annual money, resources and protections from the federal government were Indians, and that was intended to be temporary until Indians could be full citizens which came with the Snyder Act of 1924. Tribes enjoy all the technology and resources provided by Young Man, the Settlers and their descendants...to this day! It's why their reservations thrive at all.

Nothing within the four corners of the U.S. Constitution includes tribal governance, tribal sovereignty or any aspect of federal Indian policy. Congress has power over Indian commerce, nct Indian tribes. Justice Clarence Thomas put a powerful challenge out to his colleagues on the Bench, and to Congress. Here are his clear words:

> "Congress purported [alleged] Plenary Power [all-encompassing] over Indian tribes rest on even shakier foundations. No enumerated power—not Congress' power to "regulate Commerce. . . with Indian Tribes," not the Senate's role in approving treaties, nor anything else—gives Congress such sweeping authority...And, until the Court rejects the fiction that Congress possesses plenary power over Indian affairs, our precedents will continue to be based on the paternalistic theory that Congress must assume all-encompassing control over the "remnants of a race" for its own good."
>
> — Justice Clarence Thomas, *U.S. v. Bryant*,
> No. 15-420, U.S. Supreme Court, 06-13-2016

Terms like *aboriginal rights* and *time immemorial* are political propaganda. Anything *pre*-constitutional or *extra*-constitutional is *un*constitutional...or we have no Constitution. The Constitutional priority tree of sovereignty goes like this:

1. Citizen (Popular Sovereignty, Inalienable rights).

2. State sovereignty (remember the States created the federal government).

3. Federal sovereignty (enumerated (limited) powers).

Why is the Constitution turned on its head, and why are federal, state and local elected officials so persuaded that tribal sovereignty is now superior to all other sovereignty in this country? Follow the money and follow political correctness. No elected official wants to be called "racist." No elected official wants to be taken out of office by a tribally funded challenger.

Across the Western states our federal senators, state legislators, county commissioners—too many behave as though their primary allegiance is to tribal governments. The federal "trust" relationship with Indian tribes created by the Supreme Court (1823-1830) may never supplant the trust relationship that every elected official takes to the U.S. Constitution, including specifically the first eleven Amendments.

Wake up, Washington. In 1974 the Supreme Court ruled that tribal governments are "political" and **not** "race-based" entities. (*Morton v. Monca*) This ruling was a travesty and will eventually get overturned.

We all have the right, even the duty, to challenge government decisions that impact our daily lives, our communities, our states and our country. Hopefully this book will grow the voices of citizens urgently working for the return of One Nation Under God.

Occupants of public office love power and are prone to abuse it.

— George Washington

CHAPTER 15

Stealing (Federalizing) Montana and Other State Waters

Here is a threat to the farm and cattle community coming to Western States. I recently identified ten major legal flaws of a proposed Tribal Water Compact (Montana Water Protection Act, S. 3019), and identified them as the principle beliefs of Montana Senators Steve Daines and Jon Tester. I would also include that these beliefs are supported by Montana Governor Steven Bullock, Attorney General Tim Fox, and a majority of the Montana Legislature. All of these elected officials have completely abandoned the state protections of Montana residents living in eleven counties of Western Montana. Below are the Ten Flaws of the proposed Confederated Salish-Kootenai Tribe (CSKT) Water Compact, with a few supportive examples affirming that the proposed CSKT Water Compact is entirely illegal:

1. **The U.S. Constitution is Irrelevant.** Article IV provides full faith and credit to States, full privileges and immunities of citizens, and no new "states" created within a state. Governor Bullock signed away the First Amendment of Montana citizens, and executed an intentional violation of the Fifth Amendment (takings without compensation). Bullock ignored the power of the State of Montana under the Tenth Amendment and removed the civil rights protections of Montanans under the Fourteenth Amendment, among other U.S. Constitutional violations.

2. **The Montana State Constitution is Flexible.** The CSKT Water Compact tramples upon Article II and Article IX of the Montana State Constitution by removing the popular sovereignty and inalienable rights of Montana citizens, taking water rights attached to property deeds, and transferring off-reservation Montana waters to federal "trust" for an Indian tribe. Article IX requires "a clean and healthful environment in Montana for present and future generations." Water is livelihood, or the lack of livelihood on land. Transferring authority over Montana waters to an Indian tribe that has no duty to Montana landowners is abhorrent.

3. **The CSKT Tribal Constitution is Insignificant.** Article VI of the CSKT Constitution declares that the Tribal Council's powers and duties are subject to any limitations imposed by Statutes of the Constitution of the United States. (See U.S. Constitution above). Further, Article VII of the Tribal Constitution provides a Bill of Rights that is substantially violated on behalf of enrolled tribal member landowners and irrigators within the Flathead Reservation, among other Tribal Constitution violations.

4. **The U.S. Supreme Court Rulings on Water Should Be Ignored.** The *Winters Doctrine* of 1908 is a fair and just commitment to always provide water for all tribal lands, people and enterprises. The *Winters Doctrine* excludes off-reservation waters from tribal authority. The 1981 *Montana v. U.S.* ruling provides that tribal governments have no authority over non-tribal persons or properties, absent a person's consent. The 2013 ruling in *Tarrant v. Herrmann* unanimously asserted that *"States have the absolute authority over all navigable waters within lands ceded to a state upon statehood."* These are but a few of the very powerful U.S. Supreme Court rulings utterly ignored by the federal government, State of Montana and CSKT Tribe.

5 **Tribal Sovereignty Is Superior to and More Precious than State Sovereignty.** Two major tribal privileges have caused elected officials of the State of Montana to elevate tribal sovereignty over State sovereignty: 1) tribal governments directly finance incumbents and candidates. No other American governments may do so. Indian reservations place polling precincts on federal "trust" land, where the Secretary of State has no access or enforcement authority and cannot ensure fair election practices. Elected officials benefitting from these two egregious election conditions (money and questionable tribal votes) are loath to require the Montana Legislature to end these practices. Consequently, Montana elected officials say "Yes" to every tribal whim, even to the direct harm of state sovereignty and the protection of Montana citizens.

6. **The Federal Government, State and Tribe Must Steal Water Rights Attached to Private Property Deeds.** The entire ability to implement the proposed CSKT Water Compact is contingent upon surreptitious and nefarious removal of private water rights, and ille-

gally transferring such rights to the federal government on behalf of a tribe. This is theft. This is absolute unadulterated theft of a water right without compensation, and instrumental to the success of the CSKT Water Compact. Senators Tester and Daines, Governor Bullock and their minions believe that such a travesty is a justified harm to Montana residents.

7.   **A Montana Senator's Oath of Office Must Prioritize Tribalism.** The Federal Government has a "trust" relationship with Indian tribes. States do not unless they intentionally self-impose a State "trust" relationship with Indian tribes. Montana did exactly that a couple of decades ago. See Item 5 above (candidate funding and questionable votes) to fully understand why Montana elected officials either cooperate with tribes or get taken out of office.

8.   **A Territorial War Power Against the State of Montana is the Right Way to Implement a Tribal Water Compact.** On Page 2 of the Enrolled Bill (S. 262) passed by the Montana Legislature is the following: "The Secretary of Interior…has authority to execute this Compact…pursuant to 43 U.S.C. 1457…." This statute is a Territorial War Power that may be applied in federal territories, but never against a State. Montana elected officials either naively or intentionally agreed to this travesty. There has been no discussion or action by state officials to protect state sovereign authority specific to this Compact.

9.   **Montana State Legislature is Subservient to a Senator's Decisions.** Montana Legislature's bill, S. 262 was wrapped into and substantially amplified in Senator Tester's Compact Bill, S. 3013, and later in S.3019, expanding tribal authority over Montana waters and adding multi-millions to the Compact, beyond what the Montana

Legislature approved. Senators Daines and Tester overruled and exceeded the decisions of the Montana legislature, with no complaint from Montana elected officials. Fortunately, Tester's S. 3103 died in a Senate Committee in the last (not current) Congress. It has now been significantly expanded in S. 3019 by Senator Tester and/or Daines.

10. **Montana Waters Should Rightfully Be Owned and Managed by the Federal Government.** The proposed CSKT Compact transfers the state's authority over its waters in eleven Western Counties to the federal government, to be held in "trust" for a single Indian tribe. Should this Compact be ratified by Congress, all other Montana Indian tribes will demand the same water benefits as the CSKT tribe. The end result will transfer all Montana waters to the federal government to be managed on behalf of Indian tribes in Montana.

This is, of course, a horror story for the State of Montana, but it gets worse. Should this unique and highly illegal tribal water compact become law, the precedent is set for all tribes in their respective states to roll out the same demands. The Federal government is using tribes as willing pawns to federalize the waters of the Western States. The proposed CSKT Water Compact is the model, or pilot project to accomplish this goal.

Unless State elected officials resume their duty to protect State authorities and resources, the federal government and tribes have smooth sailing for dismantling the balance of power between the federal government and states. Water is life on the land. Tribal financing of elected officials is greasing the skids to get this done on behalf of a continuously overreaching federal government.

Ours is a government of checks and balances.
The Mafia and crooked businessmen make out checks, and the politicians
and other compromised officials improve their bank balance

— Steve Allen

CHAPTER 16

The Tester-Abramoff Magic Money Machine

Fertilizing the Swamp in Washington D.C.

J ack Abramoff is the lobbyist who is now a convicted felon. Senator Jon Tester was questionably elected in 2006 and continues to serve in the Senate. Almost fifteen years ago the public was overwrought in righteous anger over shenanigans of the politically corrupt Washington D.C. lobbyist Jack Abramoff. Mr. Abramoff was accused of fleecing a tribal government of over $80 million dollars. No one questioned why a single tribe would have a lose $80 million to throw at a single lobbyist. Certainly no county governments in our country have that kind of chump change to represent *their* voices.

In 2005 the public was entirely unaware that a federal money-wheel had been intentionally installed upon which many people like Abramoff—including Indian tribal leaders and elected officials continue today to personally and excessively profit. In 2020 that entire mechanism remains in place today—a nifty, enormous and continuous flow of tribal money from 574 tribes buying elected officials and lobbyists.

At least two presidential administrations helped to engineer and maintain the political climate in Washington D.C. where people like Abramoff and his partners thrived.

Abramoff didn't operate in a vacuum, nor was all of his activity illegal. In fact, most of his political fundraising and money distribution to elected officials in hopes of gaining political influence for himself and his clients was quite legal.

The timeline below illustrates the intentional federal construction of legislation and regulations that legitimized the perpetual money-moving scheme for guys like Abramoff and Tester:

October 17, **1988**: Congress passed the Indian Gaming Regulatory Act.

May 19, **1998**: Executive Order 13084, signed by President Clinton established a Tribal Office in over 25 federal agencies to expedite all tribal requests.

Jan. 28, **2000:** Federal Election Commission (FEC) Advisory Opinion No. 1999-32 declares that a tribe acting as a federal (utilities) contractor may (unlike any other federal contractors) make political contributions as "a person."

May 15, **2000:** (FEC) Advisory Opinion No. 2000-05 declared that tribal governments are not governments for purpose of election contributions. This was just in time to amply fund Bush/Gore Presidential election needs.

June 1, **2000:** Abramoff purchases (albeit fraudulently) the Sun Cruz ("Cruise to Nowhere") offshore Florida floating casinos.

September **2000**: Abramoff achieves top political power.

May **2001**: The Coushatta Tribe of Louisiana and other tribes hire Abramoff, who collects approximately $82 million by 2004.

March 27, **2002:** President Bush signs the McCain-Feingold Campaign Finance Reform Act that intentionally excluded "Indian Tribes" from disclosing contributions.

February **2002:** The poverty riddled Tigua Tribe in El Paso, Texas, provided $4.2 million in fees to Abramoff to help re-open its casino that Abramoff had helped close.

March 6, **2002:** A single tribe, the Coushattas of Louisiana (one of 574 federally recognized tribes) cuts over 60 large checks to Congressional elected officials.

March 14, **2005**: FEC Advisory Opinion No. 2005-01 declares that tribal governments, even while acting as federal contractors or associated with federal contractors may continue to make political and election contributions. (To his credit, FEC Commissioner Michael Toner vigorously dissented.)

March 14, **2005:** Thanks to the FEC, Indian tribes are governments when in need of federal funds or special preferences, but for the American election process, they are *not* governments nor federal contractors, so revenue from tribal government general funds and casinos are available for unreported, unaccountable, and unlimited influence in local, state and federal elections.

November 2006: Jon Tester narrowly defeats former Montana Senator Conrad Burns by late arriving votes from tribal reservations, secured at polling precincts on federal Indian trust land, where the Secretary of State has no oversight, authority or enforcement. This senator's questionable election changed the power in the Senate from Republican to Democrat.

The Indian Gaming Regulatory Act (IGRA) of 1988 secured an escalating tribal gaming revenue industry that exceeded 27 billion annually by 2005. The oversight agency, National Indian Gaming Commission (NIGC) justifies tribal campaign contributions and payment to lobbyists and elected officials as tribal "economic development."

It is interesting to note that a mere unelected "advisory" commission, the Federal Election Commission (FEC), appointed by the President's Executive Branch, could publish *advisory* opinions having the force of the rule of law across the country.

Three FEC Opinions opened wide the financial faucets that converted tribal governments entities into *persons* for purpose of unlimited campaign contributions, even as many tribal governments also serve as federal contractors.

No other government (state, county, municipality) nor federal contractor (i.e. public utilities) may financially contribute to America's election processes. The FEC intentionally created a special preference for Indian tribes that lured, if not openly invited, entrepreneurs such as Abramoff to jump into action to facilitate large, continuous, and secret election contributions from Indian tribes. Since tribal governments are not subject to the same federal or state campaign finance reporting requirements, substantial tribal political contributions are even the more desired and empowered.

The FEC is a quicker, smaller, more quiet and efficient resource for constructing an uneven financial playground for America's elections than the more cumbersome Congress. And the greatest financial beneficiaries to such inequity are Congress themselves, as well as Governors, and state legislators, etc. There is little to no political incentive to dismantle this money machine among elected officials that continue to receive the benefits.

Mainstream media was awash with ever-surfacing news of how Abramoff clients and funds received were redirected as contributions to elected officials, all made possible through FEC Advisory Opinions and the intentional omission of "Indian tribes" from the McCain-Feingold "reforms."

However, before the public sympathizes with the Indian tribes who were allegedly defrauded, here are a few basic questions:

- How does an Indian tribe that receives annual millions in tax-payer-federal funds, and whose tribal families continue to live below poverty level or in squalor, justify kicking in multi-millions of dollars annually to a single D.C. lobbyist?

- Why have Congress, the F EC, National Indian Gaming Commission, and Bureau of Indian Affairs silently approved tribal gambling funds derived under the IGRA to be spent on lobbyists and election campaigns as legitimate "economic development?"

- If the intent of IGRA was to promote economic development and improve the quality of life for tribal members on reservations, how have lobbyists of Abramoff's ilk, or elected officials like Tester, or tribal leaders accomplished this?

- Shouldn't tribal government decisions regarding use of their gambling revenue also be subject to just a teensy bit of input from tribal members or oversight scrutiny?

Abramoff and his partner, Michael Scanlon, were simply the first lobby-ists caught abusing a federal election system that begs for abuse. Isn't it naive to consider that they are the only lobbyists so engaged?

There are no clean hands in this dirty business. As foul as the stench of Abramoff's conduct was, the hands of all who participated in his schemes are equally odious; that includes elected officials and their staff, other lob-byists and tribal leaders — all are equally as culpable as Abramoff. There is no excuse for Jack Abramoff. He could not possibly, however, have accom-plished what he did without equally malevolent participants and co-con-spirators, some of whom still serve in elected office today.

Lastly, someone at the Executive or Congressional level of govern-ment should clearly insist that the Federal Election Commission revisit its "Advisory Opinions" regarding tribal government campaign contributions, or in the alternative, investigate the influence behind such egregious FEC decisions that have escalated 574 tribal governments political and financial power that is specifically disallowed to all other American forms of govern-ment. Otherwise, this private, unknowable piggy bank remains available to all elected officials willing to pimp for tribal governments.

Little known, seemingly innocuous FEC opinions have effectively enabled federally recognized tribal governments to purchase whatever influence they desire. The mere 50 state governments, unable to participate in elections at *all*, are clearly under siege. Voters reliant upon their respective States for clean and fair election processes have been entirely sold out.

Until gaming tribal governments are restricted in the same manner as all other American and foreign governments respecting lobbying and elections, it is not enough to just throw out one "baby," Abramoff. We must also throw out the corrupt money "bathtub" that continues to breed and feed these political predators. The opportunity for little brown sacks of unreported cash going to lobbyists, candidates and incumbents most certainly exists.

It is no wonder that numerous federal elected officials, state governors and legislators now behave as though tribal "sovereignty" is superior to and supersedes the sovereignty of the states these elected officials serve. Tribal sovereignty is not found in the U.S. Constitution. Every expansion of tribal authority over state natural resources, state lands and non-tribal citizens is a direct reduction of state sovereign authority.

Tribal governments have no authority to take such actions on their own. It is the coin-operated lobbyists like Abramoff and elected officials like Tester that we put in office, that do it for them. How much longer will the Forgotten Man and Woman tolerate this?

SECTION THREE

Other Voices

NOTE: Below is a contribution from a very courageous enrolled tribal woman in Oklahoma, whose anonymity must be preserved for fear of retribution.

CHAPTER 17

An Oklahoma Tribal Woman's Story

"Sometimes too much freedom to do as you will, to whomever you want, whenever you want, without any fear of repercussions, results in Malfeasance."

PREFACE

I am a Native American wife, mother and grandmother, and I live in Oklahoma. I am a descendant of one of our tribes' greatest chiefs of all time. He was documented a great warrior and known for his great tactical decisions in many battles like his father. He signed the Treaty of Greenville in 1795, and also 11 later treaties during his leadership. He was a highly respected intelligent chief and as a war chief to Tecumseh during the Tecumseh uprising.

In the late '70s and '80s, our tribal leader was very eloquent, and as a young motivated man, gave his speech telling tribal members, as I recall said: "we deserve better from our government and they will pay for what they did to our forefathers!" as the tribal "Pow Wow" was held, year after year, more authority, better buildings, and more services to tribal members were increasing. Tribal candidates had fierce tribal political elections. I remember well, when our leader declared at the "homecoming" in the 80's, "I will lead our people to better opportunities, financial inheritance, and become a tribe that others will envy!" I was amazed, and impressed by what he promised, and I certainly had no idea what he envisioned, nor how he planned to get us there!

At this juncture in our tribe, members began to obtain high educational degrees in the fields of law, science, environment, security, Information Technology, administration, business and anything else available to operate their envisioned community. My point is, the Federal Government obviously had no idea that tribal members around the United States were gaining high level educations and would eventually infiltrate government operations, enabling them to not only build their own empires, they would do it off the back of America. These divisive educated members soon became tribal administrators and leaders, and the rest is history!

Tribal leaders educated themselves to push back against the Federal Government. The Feds gave them more freedom to run their tribes, gaining more and more government funds, without governmental oversight. At this point, our tribal leader and his staff, re-crafted the tribal constitution. It was perfectly customized for what he was aiming to achieve. His ingenuous plan included his own police department, (Security), economic development (Financial Planners), museum (Historical Government Information on his tribal ancestry), housing programs (Residential Construction), Concrete Business (Federal Street Funds, infrastructure maintenance funds from Feds), (daycare centers (Federal Assistance for poor tribal children's tuition or matching funds), fully manned medical clinic facilities (Federal monies to help maintain these services to tribal members). They purchased a bank (giving them access to any and all private commercial or residential bank accounts and all the unauthorized use of personal information of tribal members and non-members they wanted to access,) and throw in the largest money maker for them, gambling casinos, not to mention an entire Legal and Court System, including a judge and a tribal supreme court. (Their tribal court system ran off their rules, not the federal court system.)

Now, as in most tribes, the entire legal staff and both courts are made up of 100% tribal membership. Think about that! If an employee(s) within this tribe does not carry out the demands and directives given them by their leader(s), they will lose their jobs, one way or another. They are bound to the loyalty of its leader(s) whether or not what they order is lawful or not in the eyes of the Federal Court Systems. Why would they worry, they answer to no one!

Through the years, He assembled his dream and put it into action. The Federal Government, in order to appease the now intelligent leaders, who are pushing for more and more freedoms from the Federal Government, decree that if these leaders can qualify for levels of self-sufficiency, their tribe would be renamed a Tribal Nation. It is all paperwork, and the now, educated leaders goals was to gain the Tribal Nation title.

The definition of a **tribe** is "an ethnically, culturally and religiously united social group which is largely homogenous in nature and isn't restricted to any geography or a political union". But the definition of a **nation** is "political, economic and usually military union of a large group of people set in a specific geography that may be diverse or homogenous in its demography. **(b)**

What was once a small tribe, is now a large, wealthy, multifaceted tribal nation, usually led by the same person for over 30-40 years. There are NO TERM LIMITS and tribal members are blinded by all the programs their leaders are being handed! All looks wonderful on the outside, but on the inside, absolute vengeance burns. Maybe his dream was to build himself a life fit for a king. A Kingdom! Somewhere along the line, greed took over, as well as vengeance, against those who disagreed with him or his companions. As tribal nations transform like this, usually built in the same manner, each, under one leader for a long period of time, most have turned into a "**Mafia**". **(h)**   I stated earlier that had I known how this "**Tribal Mafia**" as I refer to them now, would exist in the future, I would never have enrolled my son as a tribal member.

INTRODUCTION

As a baby, my mother and father were members of two different Indian tribes. My mother enrolled me as a member of one of the tribes. I grew up proud of my tribal heritage and was very happy to tell people of my Indian heritage. In my adult years, I followed tradition and enrolled my baby son as a tribal member. *However, I had no idea about the future, nor what anguish and heartbreak it would bring to our family. I never dreamed that enrolling him as a member of a tribe would destroy our lives.* Who would! I was a wife and young mother. I had no reason to question what was happening between tribes in the US and their neighboring cities and rural communities. I had no idea of the Federal Court issues with tribes.

Terrorized and Abused by the Tribal Mafia

Our story started over 5 years ago. A marriage that had a wonderful beginning, and ended up being an experience through hell. A co-leader in this Tribal Mafia, is the grandmother of my sons' ex-wife. Our story begins as my son's marriage ended in divorce. He worked at the same job before he married, and since his wife didn't work, it became a financial necessity that he worked an average of 60 to 70 hours a week. Working long hours didn't leave much family time. He begged her to get a job and help him with finances, so they could have more time together as a couple and a family. They were a young couple with a small baby. Financial problems and other issues started to creep in, as did other issues when new little ones change lifestyles. Thousands of couples their age end up separating and divorce. They had irreconcilable differences, and she moved out. She moved in with her grandmother, a tribal administrator. She filed for divorce in tribal court.

Tribal Court — Judge begins to tear away the child from the father's side of family.

In the three months waiting on the first court hearing, his ex-had not let him spend any time with his daughter and would not allow him to talk to her on the phone either. That also means that I, the grandmother, wasn't allowed to see or talk to her either. Our hearts were breaking, and I knew my son could barely keep it together, he missed his baby girl as did I!

At the first court hearing, my son was allowed visitation 2 nights a week and every other weekend. This was heaven! It was another couple of months until the actual court hearing date. He was so glad to get to see his daughter. I was thrilled to be able to hold and sing and talk to that precious girl! It was a terrible time as my son stayed in their marital home trying sell it, and additionally to protect it from burglars. He worked long days and came home to an empty sad house. The realtor had several showings, but no offers were made. Sadly, they ended up losing it to foreclosure. So, now, my son lost his marriage, his child, and now his home. My heart was breaking for him. He could no longer afford all the expenses falling on his shoulders, and his credit was ruined. It was all closing in on him.

Collusion — Prior to court, the Tribal Administrator participated in a private meeting with the Judge in his Chambers. (e)

We were sitting in courtroom, waiting on the judge to enter. The door from the judges' chamber opened. Looking up, we saw my sons' ex-wife, her best friend, and her attorney walk into the courtroom and take their seats.

Yes, from the Judges' Chamber! The door closed behind them and the judge still didn't enter the room. After a 10-minute delay, the judge was in a loud conversation as he entered the courtroom headed to his bench. The Tribal Administrator, grandmother of my son's ex-wife, was loudly announcing her directives to the judge. She looked out at the court and saw us looking at her. With an ugly sneer on her face and her nose in the air, she turned and closed the door. She stood in the doorway spouting long enough for us to know she had just given her orders to the judge.

Malfeasance — Tribal Administrator directed the Judge on exactly how he was going to run this court!

The judge opened the court in his usual manner, but abruptly stopped himself and stated "Well, I've got my marching orders, so we best get started." In the next breath, he announced he had already made the decision as to child's custody. He gave sole custody to the ex-wife. My son's attorney stood and started to speak. The judge shook his head and told my him "He would not hear any further discussion on the matter, and he had his mind set on it." My son's **2nd Amendment Right** was denied by the court.

Malfeasance and Defamation of Character gainst my son

My son's attorney asked the Judge if the he would allow the Court appointed Guardian Ad Lignum to give her report and testify in court as to her recommendations? He mentioned that he was under the impression that she was going to suggest joint custody. He told the judge that the report he saw had nothing in it like what the judge was exhibiting. The judge got angry and made it clear stating "**The GAL only gives her opinion and HE makes the decision.** Full dis-regard for the purpose of the GAL in a Family Law Case. **Malfeasance** continued to be apparent through the obvious orders given to the judge by the tribal administrator, directing the Judge on what his mission was! (c) The judge committed both **Malfeasance** of his position, and **Defamation of Character against my son.** (g) The result of this decision also changed my son's visitation to every other weekend, and two weeks in the summer. It is hard to share your child with your family when you only have your child 8 days a month, and just 66 days a year! Their goal was to tear our granddaughter away from my son and our family!

The next court hearing — Child Support

After several months, court convened again. At this hearing, the judge was to determine the amount of child support my son would be paying monthly to his ex for his daughter. The judge was conflicted about the type of pay stubs my son submitted to the court from his employer. As a result, the judge took it upon himself to disregard my son's paystubs. Instead, he deliberately changed figures on the paperwork resulting in a $1,000.00 increase of my son's income. **THE JUDGE COMMITTED FRAUD!** Still following the directions of the tribal administrator, the judge made sure that the tribal administrators' granddaughter would receive child support that was higher than state guidelines. Additionally, the judge also ordered my son to pay daycare on top of the higher child support. The problem is, **the child was no longer in tribal daycare, she was attending Pre-K in public school. Racketeering** was performed through this Judges' action. (d)

Judge committed Fraud, Racketeering and Collusion to commit Conspiracy.

Following this hearing, my son contacted tribal child support services requesting a review. He also notified them his daughter wasn't in daycare and they had been charging him for over a year and she wasn't in daycare, she was in public school. The person told him he needed to call his ex and she would have to call them to request the change review. **He followed their**

orders, called her and told her what they said. She laughed at him and hung up!

Nothing to be done. It was a conspiracy and they knew there was nothing he could do. They gave him the run-a-round. The next hearing was 4 months away. He could not get tribal child support services to change it and his ex would not do what they said she needed to do to notify them of the change. **His ex-committed fraud herself** by not doing what she was supposed to do.

Judge committed Fraud, Racketeering and Collusion to commit Conspiracy

We have documented references to a Secret Meeting, held by the judge, that included the ex-wife, her attorney, tribal child support services representative and the court appointed representative, in purposeful plot to financially destroy my son. "Conspiracy" meeting.

Two months later, a secret meeting was conducted between the Judge, the ex-wife, her tribal attorney, the attorney for the Child support Services, and the Court Appointed representative of the Child Support Services. (**neither my son nor his attorney was notified of it nor invited**) At the conspiracy meeting, the judge signed a court order, directing my son to pay the ex-wife for the daycare he was fraudulently charged. This was never changed by the court nor the tribal child support services after several official notifications. **(e) The child was in public school for those 2 years, and she wasn't in daycare.** The amount of the Court Order the judge signed, for my son to pay to his ex-wife was over $7,000. The question here pertains to Fraud, or Racketeering, because if the tribal daycare was reporting that my grandchild was attending daycare, and they were receiving federal funds for her being there when she wasn't, that probably falls under *Federal Embezzlement Charges*! If only we had the tools to prove what they had done!

There were several court hearings after this one, about general property division stuff, but my son's attorney made it clear in those hearings, that the figures the judge used were unlawful and fraudulent. He asked the judge to change the hard figures because his daughter wasn't in daycare but in public school. The judge told him my son would have to go to tribal child support services to get it changed. He wasn't going to change anything!

One delay after another, and 3 years back and forth on issues by his ex's attorney, it was very clear there was a reason the tribal administrator had been in the Judge's Chambers. Malicious Malfeasance (c) was and is still being conducted by the tribal administrator, as well as their tribal legal staff. They have performed illegal, unjustified and harmful wrongdoing which violates public trust. In Addition, they are performing Racketeering, committed through coercion, obtaining money by intimidation and force in the courtroom. (d)

Tribal Supreme Court Appeal

This case was Appealed to the Tribal Supreme Court. (Remember, all members of the supreme court are tribal members, whose oath is to the tribal leaders.) The Supreme Court overturned the child custody and they went to court again. However, he was lured into a new agreement, with the advice of my son's attorney, to agree to New custody rules. It was to drop child support and also stopping the daycare charges. However, my son would have to agree to help pay ½ of all of the future school activities and miscellaneous events that their daughter played or was active in. So, my son's attorney, without hearing the GAL give her report, guided my son to sign the new agreement, but the sole custody remained with her mother. The agreement was struck in court in 30 minutes. The judge would not hear anything on the Court Order action about the past due child support that wasn't due. It was fraud! (**f**) In addition, the Court Ordered that he pay his ex-wife ALL of his retirement, not the amount he was directed to pay in the original divorce decree. The amount ordered was over 5X's the amount named in the original divorce decree, Big difference! (**c**). **Plot thickens, and Malfeasance by the court governed by the tribal administrator. Conspiracy proving itself.**

More Conspiracy activities

There have been fraudulent attempts utilizing the bank owned by the tribe. Impersonating the government by attempting to place a Levy on my son's bank account. Also, on his current wife's bank accounts, using fraudulent documents, and not following proper procedures. The bank did freeze their bank accounts! However, while at his bank, he was assisted in obtaining a phone number and contacted the right services for very enlightening information. With the help of his bank representative, they noticed that the person(s) conducting the fraud, did not follow proper banking procedures. He followed all guidelines to get the Levy released, and was successful. However, the bank still had to continue holding the funds until the child support services notified them to stop the Levy.(**f**) It was totally obvious that this harassing event was now Machination, carried out by someone who holds access to a bank and has some knowledge of how Levy's are done through a Child Support Services, like Oklahoma Dept. of Human Services. We know that the best friend of my son's ex-wife has exactly that type of experience, and she recently started working for the tribal administrator! Coincidence or Conspiracy!

This tribal leader, their tribal court system, as well as employees working for them in the bank they own, and employee(s) who previously worked for the Oklahoma Department of Human Services (ODHS), had <u>impersonated a Federal Agency</u> by using ODHS blank forms and forged the name of the Tribal Child Support Services, and has committed Collusion, Fraud, Malfeasance, Extortion and Defamation of Character against my son.

Tribal Immunity!

We have been in this court battle for over 5 years now, and I know we have spent over $25,000.00 fighting them. Every time my son's ex files a Motion in Court about whatever she wants, costs us $2,000 for an attorney. However, you can't fight someone who answers to no one and can do whatever they want, whenever they want to whomever they want and never be held accountable for their actions. Tribal Leaders Know This! It is their "Modus Operandi"

"Tribal Mafia" actions are obvious, and will continue
unless Congress Removes Immunity from all tribes in the United States.

I have spent this last year, working to gain the ears of Congressional Representative across the United States, taking our case as an example, as well as over 20 other cases, whose families have been torn apart, financially devastated and literally ended up destitute as a result of a tribal courts and their judges. Tribal Lobbyists are deep into the pockets of Congressional leaders. The sad part is, they are the only ones with authority to remove the Immunity. Unless congressional members are educated about what having Immunity does to all U S Citizens, they are blinded by the lobbyists, who will keep them dumb!!!

My son's divorce case was the result of vengeance from the tribal administrator and her granddaughter. The tribal administrator used all of the tribal power and authority and entities under the auspices of the tribe, to build and plot against him. The Administrator used tribal employees, tribal court and tribal supreme court system, to take every dime he has, as well as mine! Had my son been able to refuse going through the tribal court system and had a choice to go through federal court in his divorce hearings, none of this mafia type activity would have happened. He would have been allowed his constitutional rights of representation and never would have been treated the way he was. I'm not saying federal courts are always right, I'm saying they are not tainted by tribal leaders, who have superiority over them.

My son now has a blended household of 6. The company my son worked at 14 years was sold, and his position was done away with. He lost his job on top of everything else he lost in these last several years. He is not afraid of work, and has been doing anything he could to help earn enough money to provide food, a home, clothes and pay a mortgage and utilities on top of that. It is outrageous that he has to pay the fraudulent monthly court ordered amount of $700,

HARRASMENT — Continues

Recently, he was served with another harassing Motion.

Any whim or mad tantrum his ex gets, she calls her tribal attorney to file a motion, and tells him to add on it my son can pay her attorney fees. Manipulation by his ex-wife is also harassment. The following probably sounds familiar to you that have harassing exes.

His ex-wife schedules ballgames for every weekend of his visitation schedule. In the summer, she schedules out of town ball tournaments ensuring that my son's wife and the rest of their family cannot spend time doing other things families do in the summertime. She manipulates their lives through her daughter and the wording the Judge placed on the divorce decree. His wife and family can't spend any family weekend outings because the judge threatened my son in court that he had better do what is directed in the decree, or he would remove his visitation completely. So, they have to do what she schedules or he would be held in contempt of court by the tribal judge.

From that day in court when the tribal administrator looked at us from the Judges Chamber door, after she had given her directions to carry out the destruction of my son's life and separate him from his daughter We fought with all we had, our time, our money, our tears, our hearts! Our resolve to pray for fairness, but there was none.

They committed Malfeasance, Collusion, Fraud, Conspiracy, Defamation of Character, blocked his 14th Amendment Rights to a fair trial, blocked his 6th Amendment right to be heard in a court of law, as they devised a conspiracy to do whatever it takes to take my son's daughter away from him, one way or another. It is very clear that this was the original plot of the conspiracy from the beginning. They secretly devised to accomplish an evil or treacherous end.

If our great ancestor Chief Topinabee was here now, he would not be happy with the way this tribal mafia operates the tribe, especially against his own people.

We have all the audio and certified court minutes that prove what they have done to my son, and safely locked away. An attorney told me, unless a tribal employee who was directed by the tribal administrator to carry out the directives of the plot, or was a member of this conspiracy, or unless someone is a witness and will testify to those fraudulent actions, we can't go to trial. We must have physical proof of their fraudulent actions, as with false daycare records showing she was in school and that they requested federal funds for those days. Because we can prove she was in public school. We would have to prove they would have received federal funds and misused federal funds. Could those funds have gone to my son's ex-wife instead? If anyone could or would step forward with any viable proof that would stand up in a federal court of law, I would find a way to pay them their worth!

My heart hurts, my whole-body weeps, and has fought this battle with everything I physically, emotionally and financially have. My son has suffered so much, that he said it feels like they have taken a knife and cut out his heart! He doesn't want to even entertain the thought that he would have to give up his daughter. Ultimately, they have left him no other choice.

He cannot continue life like he has this last 5+ years. He doesn't have it in him. Neither do I. We are drained of everything. Fear found its way inside me as I talked to my son about all of this living hell we have been through. He has spoken about it as though it were part of his possible answers to his hurting, but Suicide is not an answer. I just pray that he never lets that thought crawl into that dark space of his mind ever again. It appears that in order for my son to be able to live some semblance of a life without being manipulated and harassed, drained of every dime he makes, and never knowing when another motion will be filed at the whim of his ex-wife, he will have to quit this fight. That will mean giving up his precious little girl. As I sit here writing this, I cannot stop crying because I know that we have given all we have to keep her in our lives and her mother's greed, hate and vengeance has taken her away. If there is a silver lining in all of this, we know that when his sweet little girl gets old enough, she will find out what her mother, her tribal leading grandmother, and the tribal judge did to take her daddy out of her life.

I hope and pray that I live long enough to see the day where my grand-daughter is back with us and I have the opportunity to fully inform my granddaughter, of the truth. Secretly, I would love to dance on the graves of the tribal leader, tribal judge, as well as those that were a part of the conspiracy in all of this. They clearly didn't care how it will affect my grandchild. There was nothing done in that tribal court that benefited my grandchild. It all benefited the child's mother, and possibly the tribal administrator, who may have reaped benefits in the tribal daycare funds from the Federal Supplemental Funds the tribe receives per each attending student.

Our Lord and Savior will help us move through this terrible ordeal. One day, our beautiful grandchild will hear the truth and understand she has been sorely missed and welcomed back to her place in our lives, enjoying our complete love for her as if she had been with us all along. I pray for the day to hug my sweet grandchild again, and pray to see her back with the Daddy she adores, yet, knowing exactly who caused her so much pain that took her Daddy away from her.

Please Lord, never let them forget what they have done to our sweet child, her father, and me.

> *"Sometimes too much freedom to do as you will, to whomever you want, whenever you want, without any fear of repercussions, results in Malfeasance."*

REFERENCES:

(a) From Wikipedia, the free encyclopedia *"Topinabee, Chief of the Potawatomi"*)

(b) Quora.com "Rachith Sridhar, Politically Correct. (July 11, 2015.)

(c) Malfeasance — Dictionary definition: the performance by a public official of an act that is legally unjustified, harmful or contrary to law; wrongdoing (used especially of an act in violation of public trust.)

(d) Racketeering — Dictionary definition: When an organized group (Tribal Nation) commits crimes through extortion or coercion. Attempting to obtain money or property from another person, usually through intimidation or force.

(e) Collusion — secret or illegal cooperation or conspiracy, especially in order to cheat or deceive others. (illegal cooperation or conspiracy, especially between ostensible opponents in a lawsuit)

(f) Embezzlement — Theft or misappropriation of funds placed in one's trust or belonging to one's employer.

(g) Defamation of Character is a term that is used to describe when false statement is written or spoken about an individual with the intent of harming or slandering their reputation.

(h) Mafia (merriam-webster.com / Wikipedia) — A mafia is a type of organized crime syndicate whose primary activities are protection racketeering, arbitration disputes between criminals, and brokering and enforcing illegal agreements and transactions. Mafias often engage in secondary activities such as gambling, loan sharking, drug trafficking, prostitution and fraud.

Rick Jore is a business owner in Ronan, MT. He served 4 terms in the Montana House of Representatives advocating for constitutional government and restoration of freedom. He is no fan of political expediency, political pragmatism, and party politics. He would rather be on his horse in the mountains, but has pledged, for the sake of his posterity and others, to be eternally vigilant for the cause of freedom wherever he may be.

CHAPTER 18

Between the Cruel Contradiction of Assimilation and "Tribal Sovereignty"

By Rick Jore — Ronan, Montana

Earlier this month (April 2020), a federal District Court Judge issued a decision against the county in which I live. "A rightly discarded assimilationist policy" was a phrase he used to justify his decision. An astute reader of the decision will notice the inappropriate inclusion of "rightly" as an expression of his personal opinion. Such inclusion, however, is typical of the often emotional debate that arises from the consequence of changing federal Indian policy from "assimilationist" to "tribal government sovereignty." The judge at least acknowledged the change. What is almost never acknowledged by judges and others within state and federal government, however, are those whose lives are caught square in the middle of the cruel contradiction and double-mindedness of this virtual 180 by the federal gov't.

The initial assimilation policies of the federal government culminated with the *Indian Citizenship Act* in 1924. Logically, that should have been the fulfillment of the purpose of treaties with Indian nations; for how could any sensible person assume the United States could have an Art. VI treaty with a segment of its own citizens? Ten years later however, the FDR administration — driven mostly by the agenda of statist sociologist John Collier — promoted "a new deal for Indians." Collier was appointed Commissioner of Indian Affairs in 1933 by Franklin Roosevelt and he immediately contrived *The Indian Reorganization Act.*

Sometimes referred to as the *Wheeler-Howard Act,* the IRA was passed by Congress and signed into law in 1934. It reversed decades of assimilation policies of the federal government by prohibiting "allotment in severalty to any Indian" and "restored to tribal ownership" all remaining "surplus" lands. That is to say, remaining "surplus" reservation land that had not been heretofore allotted ("severed" from the whole) to individual Indians or sold to non-Indians was "restored" to the collective ownership of the tribes. (It had to be "restored" to tribal ownership because specific allotment acts pertaining to specific Indian reservations had removed it from such ownership.)

Like so many sociologists who view government as a tool for social and economic manipulation and control rather than an instrument to secure individual rights and freedom, Collier's efforts — intended or not — restored and perpetuated the Indian people to a status of "ward of the government." By stopping allotment to individual Indians, the Act stopped the process of assimilation. The opportunity for them to become private landowners, and therefore free people, was diminished greatly and they were once again contained by a "tribal" — I would say "communal" — property ownership and lifestyle, under the umbrella of a federal government "trust" relationship.

Indeed, many saw through the IRA and opposed it, including tribes and tribal members. Alice Lee Jamison, member of the Seneca tribe of New York, Indian rights activist, and journalist was a major critic of the Bureau of Indian Affairs and the New Deal policies of commissioner John Collier.

Her testimony to the House Indian Affairs Committee in 1940, expressing the consequences of the IRA, were frank: *"In law and in fact, it (the BIA) does everything for the Indian which a guardian, duly appointed by a court, would do for any "incompetent." The Indians are held in this status of "incompetent wardship", from which there is no escape. It is a virtual status of dictatorship. Restricted or ward Indians can do nothing without the consent of the Bureau officials."*

It must be pointed out that the IRA did take into account past Congressional actions pertaining to land ownership within reservation boundaries, affirming that reservations where land had been allotted or sold to non-Indians as authorized by treaty language, *had been legally diminished.* That fact is often overlooked, neglected, or simply misunderstood.

The Act contains this provision: *"Provided, however,* That **valid rights or claims of any persons to any lands so withdrawn existing on the date of the withdrawal shall not be affected by this Act:...**" In context, "withdrawn" means taken out of/removed from the reservation. From experience, I can say that there is great confusion among citizens, both tribal and non-tribal, and elected officials about the importance of this diminishment of reservations, at least here within the State of Montana as pertaining to the Flathead Indian Reservation. (At a candidate forum in 2016 I asked the numerous legislative and county office candidates if the Flathead Indian Reservation has been diminished. Not one of them answered clearly in the affirmative. Most obviously did not understand the significance of the question.)

Therein lies "The Cruel Contradiction" which stems from this change in federal Indian policy. Both tribal members and non-tribal members within the boundaries of reservations suffer under this contradiction: Tribal citizens...the trap of paternalistic wardship; non-tribal citizens...assumed jurisdiction over them by an "authority" they have no say in; both...a diminishment of natural citizenship rights.

On the one hand, for example, the State of Montana exercises authority to tax private fee land that has been "withdrawn" from the Flathead Indian Reservation, where I live, clearly assuming diminishment of the reservation. Paradoxically, it makes agreements with the Confederated Salish and Kootenai Tribes (CSKT) of the Flathead Reservation which removes tax paying state citizens from the benefits and protection of the Montana Constitution and places them under tribal authority, clearly assuming non-diminishment of the reservation. The tribal perspective, of course, is "this is our reservation, we have 'treaty rights,'" even though their own corporate charter acknowledges that they are organized under the authority of the Indian Reorganization Act of 1934 rather than the Hellgate Treaty. Some are so bold as to publicly contend that non-member property owners "are living on stolen land" because, after all, "treaties are forever documents" and "our treaty established a permanent homeland for us."

The Hunting and Fishing Agreement between the State of Montana and the CSKT allows taxation of non-members by the tribes. It requires them to pay the tribes to hunt waterfowl and upland game birds and to fish on **private, state, and federal land** within the boundaries of the reservation. The CSKT water compact, which assumes to legally define private fee property and all county, state, and federal roads and highway rights-of-way as "reservation land," removes tax paying state citizens from the constitutionally secured and protected administration of water rights as a duty of the state by placing them under an entirely separate "Flathead Reservation Water Management Board," the members of which are determined by two votes for tribal members and one vote for everyone else. This diminishment of representation in state government for citizens who are fully taxed by that state is clearly a violation of equal protection.

The County where I live, a large part of which is tribal land not subject to taxation, currently has a Sheriff — the chief enforcer of all county ordinances and state laws — who is not legally subject to many of those laws because of his status as a tribal member. (By all accounts, he is a good man and a good Sheriff. That is not relevant to my point.) In recent years, we have had a County Justice of the Peace who was not subject to the jurisdiction of the very court over which she presided or to many of the laws which she used to pronounce judgement on fellow citizens. Currently, my State Senator and State Representative are not subject to most of the laws and taxes that they can vote to place on me and others who are not tribal members but who live and own property within the boundaries of a "diminished" Indian reservation. Violations of the foundational American principle of *The Rule of Law?* How can it not be? Anyone who cannot understand that a person cannot be properly represented by someone in a government office that is not subject to the same laws as that person simply does not understand *The Rule of Law.* (My experience as a state legislator has convinced me that, in fact, we are quite ignorant of The Rule of Law principle and we have devolved into a *Divine Right of Kings* presupposition in the legislative/policy making process.)

The solution to all this? Ronald Reagan once said: *"They say the world has become too complex for simple answers. They are wrong. There are no easy answers, but there are simple answers."*

The answer truly is simple. Freedom. For everyone. Under the same law. No more paternalistic government. No more preferential policies. Simple. Just not easy.

Bruce Elliot was born and spent his early years in Billings, Montana, where his family owned a retail furniture business. After graduating from Princeton University in 1962 with a degree in philosophy, he served 7.5 years active duty in the U.S. Navy as a commissioned line officer that included tours at sea and service in Vietnam, and 14 more years in the Naval Air Reserve at Naval Air Station Whidbey Island, Washington, retiring in 1983 with the rank of Lieutenant Commander. Bruce earned a Master's Degree in Business Administration at the University of Washington in 1972. He was employed by the Mount Vernon School District in Skagit County, Washington, as Assistant Superintendent for Business, retiring in 1996. For the past 25 years, Bruce has lived in La Conner, Washington, within the boundaries of the Swinomish Indian Tribal Community reservation.

CHAPTER 19

Is There a Solution to the "Indian Dilemma"?

By Bruce Elliot — Fidalgo Island, Washington

My friend Elaine Willman, whom I have the greatest respect for her boundless courage and unceasing determination, asked if I would contribute a few words describing tribal actions that have adversely affected Skagit County in northwest Washington State. Before addressing county issues, it is necessary to set the stage with a brief review of national and state actions and policies that affect Indian tribes, and therefore all of us. These include — but are not limited to — the Indian Citizenship

Act of 1924, the Indian Reorganization Act of 1934, and the Indian Gaming Regulatory Act of 1988.

The Indian Citizenship Act granted full U.S. citizenship rights to all American Indians. It has been argued — so far unsuccessfully — that all previous treaties with tribes should have been extinguished and nullified then and there because the U.S. government does not make treaties with its citizens. The Indian Reorganization Act reinforced the establishment of Indian reservations and emphasized the concept of "sovereignty", that tribes have the right to self-government, thus independence from federal and state controls. The Indian Gaming Regulatory Act gave tribes the monopoly rights to own and operate casinos as a means of self-sufficiency and economic independence.

Washington State is home to 29 federally recognized Indian tribes with populations ranging from fewer than 100 to more than 10,000 enrolled members residing on reservations (U.S. government lands held in trust) as small as 12 acres and as large as 1.4-million acres in area. Current census data (2019) reveals that the total American Indian population in Washington State is less than 2% of the total. However, their influence on the political landscape and thus state government is vastly disproportionate to their numbers.

For the past 25 years, I have resided on fee-simple property owned jointly by me and my wife on Fidalgo Island within reservation boundaries claimed by the Swinomish Indian Tribe, and even though it is fee property subject to county control and taxation, it mysteriously remains subject to certain tribal restrictions. (The tribe levies taxes on utilities, and in addition to the county, requires tribal approval and issuance of building permits.) Fidalgo Island is part of Skagit County, a scenic agricultural area located 60 miles north of Seattle, and is separated from the mainland at the western end of the county by a navigable waterway, the Swinomish Channel. The island is accessed by highway bridges, one of which — the aptly named "Rainbow

Bridge" because of its arched design and bright orange paint — connects the south-east part of the island to the incorporated waterfront town of La Conner with a population of about 1,000.

In basic form, all Indian reservations are federal properties, i.e. U. S Government lands "held in trust for the benefit of Indian tribes". In the case of the Swinomish and other coastal tribes in Washington, the reservation was created by the Point Elliott Treaty of 1855 by the then Washington Territories Governor, Isaac Stevens (Washington did not become a state until 1889). Article VII of the Point Elliott Treaty allowed the reservation to be divided and given to individual Indians. Early maps (circa 1900) show about 80% (my estimate) of the Swinomish reservation area was allotted. Later, some tribal members sold their allotments, many to non-Indian families such that today, the reservation is a checkerboard of tribal and nontribal land. The area where my property is located, at the very southern end of Fidalgo Island, was included in a sale of approximately 72 acres in 1884.

In 1968, a developer from Seattle negotiated a 75-year renewable lease of approximately 400 acres of raw land with the Swinomish Tribe on which he intended to build a planned residential community. The original agreement was based on the terms of a master lease arrangement that outlined a payment schedule to the tribe, and sub-lease terms to lot renters. Over time, building lots were platted, some 800 homes were constructed, and community amenities including a marina, golf course, clubhouse, and swimming pools were added. This community, known as Shelter Bay, is now home to approximately 1,700 individuals. Residents pay a rental fee for the land usage, but own the homes and other improvements constructed on that land. Until recently, property taxes for those homes and improvements were collected by Skagit County.

In 2010, in Washington's Thurston County, the Chehalis tribe sued the county over property tax collections on Great Wolf Lodge, a resort operation partly owned by the tribe constructed on reservation land. First heard in District Court, the judgment was ruled in favor of the county. The tribe appealed that decision, and in 2013 the lower court's ruling was overturned by the U.S. Court of Appeals for the Ninth Circuit in favor of the tribe, holding that the county could not tax real property, regardless of ownership, on trust land leased from an Indian tribe. Thurston County, likely for financial considerations, did not elect to further appeal the case.

The Ninth Circuit's ruling was landmark in the State of Washington and led the state Department of Revenue (DOR) to issue a "tax advisory" to all 39 county assessors in the state. The normal process for issuance of a tax advisory is for DOR to invite input and commentary from the state's county assessors prior to issuance. Not only was that not done in this case, it was later learned via a Freedom of Information Act request that tribal influence played the major role in the DOR's "advisory" action.

When the DOR's "tax advisory" landed on the desk of the Skagit County assessor, it was interpreted as tantamount to law, and action was taken to remove the majority of properties in Shelter Bay (a few are on fee-simple land) and a few similar, separate leases from the county property tax roll — a total of 931 properties altogether. That meant local taxing districts, e.g., schools, hospital, library, fire, dike, etc., would lose about $1.8 million in local tax revenue that would otherwise have been collected and distributed by the county.

This caused other "complications" regarding possible tax refund liabilities for prior year's tax collections that clouded the issue, but the major effect was to cause a shift in tax liability and rates to other taxpayers in the local taxing districts to "make up the difference" as provided for by law. This shift caused property taxes to increase by as much as 25% in one year in some cases, and a sense of shock and outrage throughout the community.

In Shelter Bay, the situation got even worse. The Swinomish Tribe saw an opportunity to fill the void created by the county's property tax withdrawal as a consequence of the Great Wolf Lodge decision and set about to establish their own "tax authority", using county-provided assessed values as the basis of their calculations. Since 2015 the Swinomish Tribe has collected a "use and occupation" tax on non-Indian Shelter Bay residents whose homes are on leased trust lands. A major and valid sore point for many is that the payers of tribal "use and occupation" taxes have virtually no voice or means whatsoever to communicate how their tax monies paid to the tribe will be used, i.e., classic "taxation without representation"!

The tribe feels no obligation that it "owes" any of the taxes it collects, including those taxes voted upon by the community specifically for schools (e.g., special levies), to the local taxing districts, preferring to negotiate "contributions" they deem reasonable to cover the various revenue losses. This has typically resulted in an annual shortfall of several hundred thousand dollars, somewhat compensated for by the "tax shift" mentioned previously. The entire system is broken, with no apparent relief in sight. But there appears to be a possible "maybe"…

Last year, Riverside County, California, appealed a property tax lawsuit in Palm Springs filed against the Aqua Caliente Indian tribe that on its face appears similar to the situation in La Conner. This appeal also was heard by the Ninth Circuit, which this time ruled in favor of the county. It is possible that this case — the only other case in the Ninth Circuit's nine western state jurisdiction that has generated any publicity — may have some bearing on the Shelter Bay situation, and numerous affected taxpayers have urged the current county assessor to seek judicial review. (After an initial consult by the Skagit County assessor with the state DOR, that agency concluded there was no similarity. The county subsequently has sought a legal opinion from the state attorney general's office that is pending.)

However, Washington residents are in a constant uphill battle when it comes to dealing with tribal matters. State political leadership has long been sympathetic to tribal interests, especially with the influx and influence of campaign money generated by tribally owned casinos. Since the passage of the Indian Gaming Regulatory Act of 1988 (IGRA), past governors have been especially generous to tribes, as has the current governor, Jay Inslee. Likely the most egregious was former governor Christine Gregoire who in 2006 benefited from $650,000 in campaign contributions from the state's Indian tribes. The trade-off was an agreement with the tribes to forego negotiating a compact with the tribes that included casino revenue sharing that would have generated revenue for the state estimated at $140 million per year! (The state did negotiate compacts with tribes per IGRA requirements, mostly in the late 1990s followed by later amendments, but sought no revenue sharing.) The stated "rationale" for her action was to "slow down" the growth of casino gambling in the state.

Twenty-six states now host one or more Indian-owned and operated casinos. Twenty-five states have negotiated compacts per IGRA that include revenue sharing from casino profits. Washington State's compacts with its tribes are the one exception. That was 15 years ago, which means that former governor Gregoire's "deal" with Washington tribes has cost the taxpayers of Washington well in excess of $1 billion in lost revenue!

Today, there are 35 casinos operated by 25 tribes in Washington State. Five of them, including the largest in the state, are less than an hour's drive from my home. The nearest, the Swinomish Casino and Lodge, is located at the north end of the reservation next to a major highway and was built on several acres of landfill in what are normally heavily restricted tide lands. The operation encompasses not only a sizeable gaming area, but now includes a major hotel with large meeting/convention/entertainment spaces and several restaurants, an RV park, tax-free tobacco and cannabis outlets, an off-site 18-hole golf course complex and gas station, an off-site health center, and multiple convenience stores and gas stations, all of which compete (tax free) with local, non-Indian businesses. Additionally, the tribe owns an apartment complex and other off-reservation properties in the town of La Conner, and operates numerous "business enterprises" including major fireworks sales and distributions, tax-free tobacco products sales and a large fishing/crabbing operation.

State governors have the power to grant exceptions to off-reservation casino locations. The current Washington governor Jay Inslee, who accepted maximum allowable campaign contributions from several Indian tribes, also gave final approval for a $400-million tribal casino to be constructed off-reservation in a Spokane suburb. No "quid pro quo" here, of course…

I believe we will rue the day Congress passed IGRA that gave tribes the monopoly rights to own and operate casinos. At the very least there should have been a "sunset" clause or review provision that after a certain level of profitability was attained — a defined means test — casinos would become taxable like any other business in the state and pay their fair share. And why do Indian tribes with successful, highly profitable casino operations continue to receive federal funding and grants (i.e., taxpayer monies) administered by BIA if they have truly attained economic self-sufficiency via IGRA, which has been in force now for more than 30 years? That was a concern Slade Gorton of Washington State posed as a member of the U.S. Senate in year 2000 that was vehemently opposed by Indian tribes and many argue cost him his Senate seat. No one has raised the question publicly since.

Tribal casinos have enormous advertising budgets for media promotions that include newspaper, radio and television, magazine and electronic (on-line) advertising. Tribal influence now extends to areas never thought possible: Washington State law now requires that Indian history and culture be taught in all public schools. And in La Conner public schools, the ancestral Swinomish language, Lushootseed, is offered as an elective class. A tribal casino, Angel of the Winds, in neighboring Snohomish County has purchased naming rights for the major public arena in the nearby city of Everett. And while sports betting is currently illegal in Washington State, tribes actively lobbied the legislature to allow sports betting exclusively in Indian casinos despite substantial competition from outside gaming interests and vocal opposition. Not surprisingly, the tribes won!

Property taxes and loss of casino revenues are not the only issues of concern in La Conner. More than half the students in the La Conner School District now reside on tax-exempt tribal reservation land (i.e., U.S. government land held in trust) which now, after the Great Wolf Lodge ruling by the Ninth Circuit, includes Shelter Bay. In Washington State, most school districts periodically seek voter approval to raise additional funds needed to pay for school operations and services not funded by the state. They do this by a school board's presenting special levy property tax proposals to the community for a vote of the people. A favorable majority vote (i.e., passage of the special levy) means that property owners agree to pay additional taxes that are distributed directly to the school district. But in La Conner, the majority of residents live on trust lands that are property-tax exempt, yet are permitted (actually, strongly encouraged!) to vote for property taxes they don't have to pay, either directly as owners, or indirectly as renters! In other words, their majority vote results in property taxes that are 100% paid by others in the community. How this travesty is considered fair or even legal is a mystery.

The Swinomish tribe has been in a unique position of power for many years. Until he was defeated in a recent election, the tribe's leader and senate chairman, Brian Cladoosby, has personally defined the tribe. Cladoosby is a charismatic and consummate politician who was first elected to the tribal senate 35 years ago, and been its chairman for the past 23 years. During his reign, Cladoosby has been president of both the National Congress of American Indians and the Affiliated Tribes of Northwest Washington that have provided him a powerful voice and political connections at both the state and national level.

The Swinomish tribe, through legal action and a cozy relationship with the state Department of Ecology, has caused water rights restrictions in the county that adversely affects farmers and land-owners who cannot drill wells, even for domestic use, as a result of the "instream flow rule" — a theoretical water resource formula designed to enhance salmon survival. (The tribe maintains that salmon are a "treaty right", and a key part of their religion and existence.) This action materially affected hundreds of property owners in the county, and adversely affected property values, severely depressing them. Subsequently, this issue has been mitigated to some extent by securing alternative water sources.

Additionally, Washington tribes, arguing on the basis of treaty rights, successfully demanded legislation that requires the state to overhaul/ upgrade hundreds of roadway culverts throughout the state to facilitate salmon spawning at a cost to taxpayers of more than $3.7 billion. The legislation was appealed by the state in Federal court (lost), then further appealed to the U.S. Supreme Court that upheld the lower court's ruling. As a consequence of this requirement and a highly-visible example, one of the culverts in the county — installed under six lanes of Interstate 5 highway that recently underwent a major overhaul took several months to complete and cost millions of dollars — serves a "salmon stream" that is dry half the year!

Under the concept of "sovereignty" which many believe is invalid and has no legal basis, Indian tribes have the sole right and authority to determine which individuals are tribal members, i.e., there is no externally prescribed definition, control process or mechanism. In short, anyone can be declared an enrolled "tribal member" at the discretion of the tribe, and according to the BIA, "who those individuals are is no one's business but the tribe's".

With fully unilateral membership discretion, it is theoretically possible to "create" an Indian tribe with few if any members with a "blood" relationship, in which case it is a total sham and a further abuse of common sense. Such was the case with the "re-creation" of the Pequot tribe in Connecticut, as described in detail by Jeff Benedict in his book, "*Without Reservation*", and Donald Mitchell in his book "*Wampum*" that includes entire chapters on "Fake Tribes" and "Fake Reservations". Quoting from "*Wampum*", page 254: "...[A] group that 'possesses powers of self-government' is called a 'federally-recognized tribe'. In 1979...there were 277 groups...the BIA [Bureau of Indian Affairs] said were federally recognized tribes. In 2015 there were 340." Per Wikipedia, as of December 20, 2019, there are now 574.

When one considers how long the "Indian Dilemma" has been a struggle for both the government and Indian tribes alike, and one wonders why, the answer boils down to one common factor: politicians. Over many decades and now centuries, politicians — sometimes with good intentions, and other times with utter self-interest, carelessness and/or disdain — created the many (and frequently conflicting) laws, regulations, and circumstances ostensibly "to benefit Indians", but ultimately to benefit themselves. In many respects, Indians and tribes were used like pawns on a chessboard, the majority deriving few if any substantial benefits, but the politicians garnering many through tribal contributions to their election campaigns, and individual tribal member votes. Today, the "Indian dilemma" is the goose that lays the golden egg...and no politician who gets that gold is going to do anything to harm that goose!

Is there a solution to the "Indian Dilemma", and will there ever be one? I was born and raised in Montana — Big Sky country with few people and lots of space — 60 miles away from the nearest Indian reservation. Like the vast majority of Americans, I had no close contact of any sort with anything Indian, and upon reflection, feel my experience fits the general attitude that has prevailed almost since the colonists first set foot in North America and the original thirteen states were formed: out of sight, out of mind. (Consider the official federal policy in the 19th century of relocating numerous tribes west of the Mississippi River…out of sight, out of mind. But over time, with increasing immigration, population growth, the building of the transcontinental railroads, the Gold Rush in California, etc., the west was no longer a sanctuary, and out of sight, out of mind became more difficult.

Growing up, my perception of Indians was rather stereotypical, and long-distance; a few sketches taken from history, "cowboys and Indians" of western movies, and a rare passing-through of Indian reservations like the Crow, Flathead and Blackfeet in Montana. My interest sharpened considerably when I settled in La Conner in the 1990s, even though I'd been living in Washington State since the mid-1960s. Even in the 1990s and early 2000s and living in close proximity to the Swinomish reservation, my attitude was arms-length — essentially a philosophy of "live and let live" — and didn't really come into focus until issues like the Great Wolf Lodge situation arose. Now I was suddenly personally affected, and began to take a real interest. I've read much of the contemporary literature on the subject, am now deeply aware that there are a lot of issues involving tribal matters — mostly unresolved — and have become increasingly curious why that is so. I've already surmised that politicians play a huge role in maintaining the status quo, as do the Indians themselves.

There is a quote attributed to Henry Ford, rightly or wrongly: "Any man who thinks he can be happy and prosperous by letting the government take care of him better take a closer look at the *American Indian*." This suggests the downside of socialism, which was the philosophy espoused by John Collier and Felix Cohen who were sympathetic to Indian issues in the 1930s

Interior Department and Indian Affairs during the Roosevelt administration and Great Depression that harkened back to Justice John Marshall's views in the 1820s regarding the political standing of Indian nations. They "romanticized" Indian life on reservations, and Cohen in particular promoted (Mitchell says "invented") the concept of "sovereignty" that persists to this day. A fundamental belief is that Indians are "wards of the state" and it is the government's obligation and responsibility to take care of them. However, that benevolent viewpoint was spawned nearly a century ago, and the world has changed dramatically.

According to recent data, there are approximately 5 million Indians living in the US today, and only about 22% of them, or about 1 million, currently reside on reservations. Given the vagaries of how "Indian" is defined, those numbers are subject to question. Some people — especially those who have been indoctrinated with a "guilt complex" — feel Indians are in some way owed reparations. Others feel the time is long past due to devise a solution that works for everyone — Indians, politicians and taxpayers. Here is an outline of my solution:

1. In lieu of maintaining what is left of actual trust lands on reservations and continuing government "reparations" ad infinitum — as would appear to be the case if nothing is done — devise a way to gift or distribute what remains of trust lands to legitimate Indians, i.e., those who have a "blood" relationship. They then will own that land, free and clear, much like the allocation models that awarded lands to individuals/families in the past. Such land becomes subject to regular assessment as to value and is taxed accordingly.

2. Any properties on that land — homes, businesses, etc., remain in the ownership of the landowner, but become taxable like any other real property. Large properties and operations like casinos convert

to tribal corporations, and also become taxable as both properties and businesses. In other words, they become liable for property and income taxes.

3. Other tribal enterprises, if any, like hotels, gas stations, smoke shops, golf courses, etc., become taxable like any other business, as do any "personal" enterprises that presently may be sheltered in some measure under reservation status.

4. Abrogate all treaties as they are no longer valid. Indians have the same rights as any other citizen, no more, no less.

5. Existing federal, state and county services, e.g., health, social, welfare, etc., will absorb any needs previously provided via tribal services.

6. Local laws, law enforcement and courts have jurisdiction, same as any other community.

7. Political contributions are now legitimized, under the same rules and regulations as any other citizen or organization.

Nothing in this transformation changes or threatens any Indian tribe's culture, language, religion or pride. All of these core values can and should be maintained as each sees fit. There is no reason nor incentive to change any of them.

Given the minority of Indians still residing on reservations — only 22% — and the diluted components of what defines an Indian today, no longer by blood or quantum, but rather extremely loose, at-will determinations as a result of inter-marriage, adoptions, or simply appointment, wouldn't a restructuring of this nature make sense?

Note: This is a truly excellent read and helpfully amplifies my brief comments on these subjects in other chapters of the book.

CHAPTER 20

Native American Tribes — Pawns of Agenda 21

By Karen Schumacher — Boise, Idaho

If there were ever any classic illustration of the federal government directly partnering with the United Nations (UN) and implementing Agenda 21, it would have to be through the use of Native American Tribes. This was accomplished in 1992 by President George H.W. Bush when he signed Agenda 21 without Congressional approval.

Agenda 21, a UN action plan for the 21st century, is also known as Sustainable Development. Special Recognition of Tribes is in each chapter; however, it is Chapter 26, Recognizing and Strengthening the Role of Indigenous People and Their Communities, that established the foundation for Tribes to be used as federal government pawns. This foundation essentially gave Tribes increased authority in national policy and laws above American citizens by strengthening active participation and consultation that reflects "their needs and incorporating their values and traditional and other knowledge and practices". However, the underlying reason for increasing Tribal influence was for more federal control over Tribes through implementation of Agenda 21 objectives.

Since that time the UN has been building and strengthening Tribal sup-port within its organizations. In July 2000, the United Nations Permanent Forum on Indigenous Issues (UNPFI) was established as an advisory body to the Economic and Social Council, mandating discussions of indigenous issues related to economic and social development, culture, the environment, education, health, and human rights. Other UN bodies that deal specifically with Indigenous issues are the Special Rapporteur on the rights of indig-enous peoples (SPRRIP) established in 2001, and the Expert Mechanism on the Rights of Indigenous Peoples (EMRIP) established in 2007. These groups essentially scrutinize countries for implementation of Indigenous rights, including the United States.

Tribal non-governmental organizations (NGO) such as the National Congress of American Indians (NCAI) partner with the UN and actively engage in implementing UN Agenda 21 objectives. Through the World Conference on Indigenous People, official permanent status was given to Tribal Nations and encouraged government recognition of the "contribution of indigenous peoples to the promotion of sustainable development." The Native American Rights Fund (NARF) is another NGO that supports UN objectives and has been instrumental in suing the federal government for millions of dollars.

The UN adopted the United Nations Declaration on the Rights Indigenous People (UNDRIP) in 2007, committing the international community "to the protection of the individual and collective rights of indigenous peoples" and giving more prominence to indigenous people "as individual players on the world stage." Through UN member states, UNDRIP is being implemented at an international level.

UNDRIP deliberately goes back into United States history, resurfacing the perceived wrongs against Native Americans, summarily declares that those injustices from years ago will never be allowed again, and reparations must be made. The UN deliberately misrepresents history to advance its Agenda 21 goals.

There are forty-six Articles in UNDRIP that basically outline international standards for Indigenous people, declaring them "free and equal", and having a "right to self-determination". Other rights include not being subjected to "forced assimilation or destruction of their culture" and not being "forcibly removed from their land", neither of which has occurred in the United States for decades. A "right to practice their culture and religious traditions" and "control their education system" are two other areas.

Perhaps the most striking aspect of UNDRIP is giving Indigenous people the "right to participate in decision-making in matters which would affect their rights", a "right to maintain and develop their political, economic and social systems or institutions", the right to the lands, territories and resources which they have traditionally owned, occupied or other-wise used or acquired, and improve "their economic and social condition". This literally gives Tribes a separate government status within the United States government. It is a government to government relationship rather than through elected representation as our Republic governs.

UNDRIP strengthens the return of land by giving Tribes the "right to redress by...equitable compensation, for the lands, territories and resources which they have traditionally owned or otherwise occupied or used, and which have been confiscated, taken, occupied, used or damaged without their free, prior and informed consent". Ignoring all compensation and agreements in Treaties from over 100 years ago, UNDRIP frames this as land that was taken and Tribes now having a right to be compensated or have that land returned to them.

However, by returning said lands to Tribes, in reality it is the federal government increasing their own land acquisition and ownership as all Tribal land is held in trust by the federal government. All resources on that land, such as water, are also taken by the federal government in that trust relationship. Over the years, even prior to UNDRIP, States have challenged the ability of the federal government to take land into trust for Tribes, but since UNDRIP these government actions have only accelerated and literally gives Native American Tribes rights above those of Americans with expanded federal government authority and control.

UN accusations that Indigenous people continue to be oppressed and mistreated could not be farther from the truth. Through legislation the United States exceeded any other country on Tribal and Native American rights, going as far back as the Indian Reorganization Act (IRA) in 1934. The IRA restored tribal ownership of lands on reservations and the return of surplus lands, provided mechanisms for self-governance, authorized a funding program that aided Tribes with these changes for their economic future, and authority to manage their own education system that strengthened cultural autonomy.

The United States did not sign UNDRIP at the time it was introduced, nor has it been signed since. In spite of the fact that the United States rejected UNDRIP and has never been ratified by the U.S. Senate, it has been incrementally implemented through presidential fiat, regulatory actions, and legislation.

In 2010, President Barack Hussein Obama declared United States support for UNDRIP and proceeded to implement UNDRIP mandates. In 2013, Executive Order 13647 established the White House Council on Native American Affairs that included inter-governmental agency coordination on Indian affairs and brought in multiple federal agencies that focused on strengthening Tribal consultation in federal policy, literally putting Tribes at the same table with the federal government. He announced to Tribal leaders in 2014 his intent to restore tribal homelands and resolve water right disputes, both commitments to Agenda 21 and UNDRIP. Under President Obama alone, over 500,000 acres of land was given to Tribes by 2016.

Donald Laverdure, Principal Deputy Assistant Secretary of the Interior for Indian Affairs, also announced to the UN support for UNDRIP in 2011. Since that time, the Department of Interior and other federal agencies have implemented UNDRIP.

The DOI strategic plan 2014-2018 actively implemented UNDRIP, meeting virtually all UNDRIP mandates, accomplished through partnerships with other federal agencies. An outline of the plan was presented to the Indian Affairs committee in 2011 and as a result federal legislation was, and continues to be, passed for implementation.

Another declaration outlined in UNDRIP is the "right to the conservation and protection of the environment and the productive capacity of their lands or territories and resources", and having "access to financial assistance". Millions of dollars have been given to Tribes by the Environmental Protection Agency (EPA) for implementing federal environmental legislation. Because of Agenda 21, these actions were already taken through the Clean Air Act (CAA) and Clean Water Act (CWA). The EPA devotes financial and technical assistance with funding to Tribes that has grown from just under $10 million dollars in 1995 to $63,343,000 million in 2019 through the EPA Indian Environmental General Assistance Program (GAP). Expanded EPA regulatory control over Tribal land gave Tribes more authority to regulate their own land over that of States.

Many U.S. Tribal non-governmental organizations (NGO) have formed partnerships with the United Nations. The National Congress of American Indians (NCAI) supports UNDRIP and is an active participant with the UN. Another UN partner is the Native American Rights Fund, which provides legal assistance to "hold governments accountable" to Tribes. NGOs who partner with the UN are obligated to implement UN objectives, including Agenda 21 and UNDRIP.

As the implementation of Agenda 21 advanced, the UN introduced Agenda 2030 in 2015. Agenda 2030, also known as Sustainable Development, is comprised of 17 Sustainable Development (SDG) goals that includes empowerment of Indigenous Peoples, inclusive and equitable education for all, and engagement of Indigenous Peoples in implementing the Agenda. Each goal has specific targets for implementation, with 73 of those targets having direct links to UNDRIP. The UN Department of Economic and Social Affairs Indigenous Peoples specifically addresses the 2030 agenda.

Although the United States Senate never signed Agenda 21 or Agenda 2030, the objectives of both are being implemented by the federal government that includes using Tribes for that agenda.

One major foundation of fully implementing Agenda 2030 is 5G, the advanced broadband for faster internet speeds and its ability to connect data together. 5G is needed for the Internet of Things agenda, which is the interconnection via the internet of computing devices embedded in everyday objects, enabling them to send and receive information. This allows full control over data, monitoring, surveillance, and society. The federal government is using Tribes as an avenue for installation. Millions of dollars, grants, and proposed legislation are advancing Tribal access to 5G broadband.

5G on Tribal land will also advance SDG 7, Clean and Affordable Energy. As part of this goal, the federal government is transitioning to clean energy such as solar and wind. Tribes are receiving $15 million dollars from the Department of Energy for the agenda to develop the necessary energy technology that includes support by the Department of Interior.

The triangular relationship between Tribes, the federal government, and the UN is how Tribes are being made a pawn in an agenda. Tribal land is held in trust by the federal <u>government</u>, giving them title to the property, which is supposed to hold that land for Tribal benefit. Instead, through an unconstitutional relationship with the UN, the federal government is implementing UN objectives on that trust land, and funding Tribes to participate.

It is also the UN predatory relationship that uses Tribes to advance their agendas. In the United States, many UN declared wrongs have been addressed. Compensation has been given for ceded land, practices of assimilation and acculturation were stopped, land was returned to Tribes, and funding to advance Tribal independence has been given for years. Yet the UN is actively pursuing alleged wrongs to inflame Tribes to be proactive in claiming retribution for those wrongs.

This triangulated relationship is destroying a beautiful culture, the foundation of a Republic, and turning their sovereignty over to a despotic organization for control.

Butch Cranford is a native of Northern California with an earlier career in the U.S. Air Force from 1969-1979. Thereafter, Butch launched a career in technology, working with the Intel Corporation from 1979 through his retirement in 2002. The Cranfords built their home in Plymouth in 1989. Since Butch and his neighbors founded No Casino in Plymouth (NCIP) in 2002, Butch has become extremely knowledgeable of the Indian Gaming Regulatory Act, and other significant Indian policy statutes. As a board member of Citizens Equal Rights Alliance since 2002, Butch also served as their Chairman from 2017 — 2019. The article below is an example of the success that a few active and educated citizens can have to preserve the economy and quality of life in the lovely community of Plymouth, located in Amador County.

CHAPTER 21

Just Business as Usual for 17 Years

By Butch Cranford — Plymouth, California

What has happened in Plymouth, California since a group of Indians calling themselves the Ione Band of Miwok Indians is a story of a small community of less than a thousand defending itself from an unethical and corrupt Bureau of Indian Affairs (BIA) Our journey into federal Indian policy began on a warm April Thursday evening at a Plymouth City Council Meeting in 2003.

The Ione Indians arrived at the meeting and announced they were going take more than 200 acres into trust to build a large Las Vegas style casino in Plymouth. According to the Indians this casino was a "Done Deal" and we could do nothing to stop it. Ground breaking in six months. A small group of citizens formed No Casino In Plymouth (NCIP) and set about finding out what we could do. 75 % of Plymouth's citizens were opposed to the casino and 84% of our County's voters were also opposed because rural Amador County (pop. ~38,000) was already host to the Jackson Rancheria Casino with a second Indian casino approved at Buena Vista for a tribe with one member.

As a group, NCIP was equipped with a score of dedicated members who knew absolutely nothing about federal Indian policy or anything about taking land into trust (fee to trust) or about the Indian gaming. We were advised to negotiate with the Indians for the best deal by several so-called Indian casino "experts". We declined that advice.

The proposed casino was receiving national headlines on all the Indian websites and in our local and regional papers, and television stations. And NCIP was contacted early in 2004 by Elaine Willman, the Chairperson Citizens Equal Rights Alliance (CERA) with an invitation to attend the CERA Conference in Washington D.C later in 2004. At our next NCIP meeting it was decided that someone should attend the CERA Conference and little did I know how my life was about to change by attending that CERA Conference.

Admittedly, that first Conference was overwhelming. I was in a room with folks from all over the U.S who really were "experts" on federal Indian policy and when I returned to Plymouth, I knew NCIP had a lot of work to do. Just learning the language and acronyms associated with fee to trust, Indian gaming, or federal Indian policy requires reading and more reading. Thousands of pages and lots of legal briefs in these 17 years since 2003. And thousands or miles traveled.

Not to be to technical but the Ione Indians were planning on using a section of the Indian Gaming Regulatory Act (IGRA) that required them to be a "restored tribe and in 2006 Associate Solicitor Carl Artman delivered an opinion that the Ione Band was a restored tribe (a tribe that had been recognized then not recognized and then recognized again) This opinion was a work of fiction since Ione has never been recognized legally, never terminated and never re-recognized. This was the first of many unethical and false documents used by the Bureau of Indian Affairs and the Ione Indians.

However, facts are stubborn things and it is a documented fact that Ione was not recognized any time prior to 1992. According to a 1992 Federal District Court Order issued in a lawsuit filed by the Ione Indians demanding the United States recognize them, the Court found Ione had never been recognized. After losing in federal court the Ione Indians began to lobby then Asst. Secretary of Indian Affairs, Ada Deer, with a host of lies about the Ione Indians. In 1994 Deer issued a memo placing the Ione Indians on a list of entities eligible to receive federal benefits. A memo with no cite to any authority, no official petition for recognition, just lies and more lies and with a memo Ione is recognized. We would learn actions like this are just unethical and corrupt business as usual at the BIA.

There was never an organized tribe or a tribal government at Ione. In 1996 the Federal District Court dismissed an Ione lawsuit against Amador County because there was no "recognizable" tribal government at Ione. None of this mattered to Officials at the BIA or Department of the Interior (DOI) as evidenced by the fictional restored lands opinion delivered by Assoc. Solicitor Artman in 2006 and by the BIA's total support for the Ione fee to trust for a casino. NCIP knew the 2006 opinion to be factually wrong and in 2008 NCIP requested DOI Solicitor David L. Bernhardt withdraw the opinion. NCIP provided him with a comprehensive memo detailing what was wrong with the opinion and in January 2009, Solicitor Bernhardt withdrew the Ione restored lands opinions because it was "wrong". This should have been the end of a casino for the Ione Indians and their fee to trust for a casino but then we are dealing with the BIA and DOI and the unethical and corrupt officials there.

NCIP thought that without the restored lands opinion there could be no casino and actually that was correct thinking on our part. We received more good news later in 2009 when the Supreme Court decided the Carcieri case and held that a tribe had to be recognized in 1934 and under federal jurisdiction in 1934 to be eligible for fee to trust. NCIP now believed that there was no way for the "not recognized in 1934" and "not under federal jurisdiction" Ione Indians to be eligible for fee to trust for a casino in Plymouth. But then there are those unethical and corrupt officials at BIA.

And true to form, the Artman "wrong" opinion is resurrected and "restored" by Solicitor Hilary Tompkins in 2011 and the Ione Indians, the BIA and DOI were back in the casino business. In May 2012, the Acting Assistant Secretary, Del Laverdure, issued a Record of Decision (ROD) for the Ione Indians 2006 fee to trust application purporting to take 12 parcels totaling 228 acres into trust for the Ione Indians using an undocumented two prong process for determining if a tribe was under federal jurisdiction in 1934. At the time, this was called the "Cowlitz" criteria and it was used from 2010 to 2014 when the Solicitor documented and formalized the "Cowlitz" two prong process in a Solicitor opinion — M-37029.

NCIP filed suit in District Federal Court in Sacramento in June 2012 challenging the Laverdure ROD. Amador County also sued and the cases were heard by the same Judge. NCIP's suit was more comprehensive and included several challenges the County chose to not include in their case. NCIP's additional challenges would be very beneficial later in our appeal to the 9th Circuit.

It took the Judge 3 years to decide our case and he granted judgement in favor of the federal defendants. NCIP and the County filed separate appeals with the 9th Circuit and in 2017 after a 30-minute hearing the 9th Circuit decided the County's case in favor of the federal defendants. However, the 9th Circuit remanded our case back to the District Court with an order to dismiss our case for lack of jurisdiction. This meant that legally our first case does not exist.

The County appealed to the Supreme Court and in October 2017 their appeal was denied. If NCIP was going to file another lawsuit we had to file before a May 24, 2018 deadline. It was discouraging to lose in the District Court and then have your case ordered out of existence by the 9th Circuit but we believed both the law and facts related to the Ione ROD were overwhelmingly in our favor. So, after serious deliberation we decided to file a new challenge and did so on May 22, 2020, two days prior to the deadline to file.

Our new lawsuit is an improved and more powerful challenge than the one we lodged in 2012 as we learned much in the past 8 years. And much has been going on at the BIA and DOI. In 2018 David L. Bernhardt was confirmed by the Senate as the Secretary of the Interior and on March 9, 2020 Secretary Bernhardt withdrew the "Cowlitz" two-part process and the M-37029 opinion because, it was "wrong". The "Cowlitz" two-part process used to approve the Ione ROD and to not decide our case was wrong and was withdrawn. Everything the BIA and DOI had used to approve the Ione ROD was wrong. All the Court had relied on to decide our case and the County's case was wrong.

So after only 17 years we are back in Federal District Court with the same Judge we had in 2012 but there are significant changes this time around. One, the NIGC in April 2020 noticed in the federal register their 2018 approval of an Ione gaming ordinance — an approval for a tribe without any land eligible for a casino which is not in accordance with the law or regulation. Two, as mentioned above Secretary David Bernhardt, withdrew M-37029 because the two-part process used to approve the Ione ROD was wrong. Secretary Bernhardt is the Solicitor who withdrew the Artman opinion because it was wrong.

Most recently the Ione Indians and their investor suddenly decided 8 years after the ROD was issued to place only 10 of the 12 parcels into trust. The investor deeded 10 parcels to the United States in trust for the Ione Band of Miwok Indians. And just to prove that the BIA will do anything, the Acting Regional Director of the Sacramento Office accepted the parcels pursuant to the Indian Land Consolidation Act (ILCA). Quite a feat as the Ione Indians are not eligible for the ILCA and Acting Regional Directors do not have authority to accept or acquire land for Indians. Only the Secretary of the Interior has this authority. Just another lawsuit waiting to happen and more unethical and corrupt business as usual at the BIA.

A written request to withdraw the 10 parcels from trust was sent to Secretary Bernhardt on April 17, 2020 and we now wait to see if he will take any action to correct the "wrong" action by the Acting Regional Director. We also await to see how the federal defendants will now defend their Cowlitz two-part process after it was withdrawn because it was wrong.

And now this last bit of information about the Pacific Regional BIA Office in Sacramento and the Ione Band. The Regional Director is a member of the Ione Band and her niece is the Chairperson of the Ione Band. Prior to becoming the Regional Director this Ione Band member was in charge of the Realty Office when the Ione Band Fee to Trust application was being processed at the Sacramento Office. Just routine unethical and corrupt business as usual at the BIA.

NCIP remains committed to there being No Casino In Plymouth but I would be remiss if I did not acknowledge how essential to our efforts these past 17 years CERA has been. I have spoken to groups all across these United States about what has happened here in Plymouth with the proposed casino and I always credit CERA for their exceptional expertise and assistance in our effort. If Elaine Willman had not extended an invitation to NCIP to attend that CERA Conference in 2004 I have no doubt that there would be large Las Vegas style casino in Plymouth today — destroying our unique rural foothill lifestyle. Thankfully, that has not happened and if NCIP can find a federal court where facts and law matter there will never be a casino in Plymouth. In the meantime, we will continue to expose the unethical and corrupt business as usual officials at the BIA, DOI, and NIGC.

NOTE: The author, Elaine Willman, has included this in the separate section of the book as a discussion about her observations and experiences while working as Director of Tribal Affairs for the courageous and persevering elected officials of the Village of Hobart, Wisconsin.

CHAPTER 22

Change in Federal Indian Policy Long Overdue

By Elaine Willman

The village of Hobart, Wisconsin, is 33 square miles of beautiful rural countryside dotted with a few high-end subdivisions. It lies to the west of Green Bay and claims numerous Packer players and coaches among its 10,000 citizens.

Hobart was incorporated in 1908 and has existed for 112 years. The Oneida Tribe of Indians of Wisconsin became a legal government in 1936 and is 84 years old. Hobart lies entirely on a *former* Oneida Indian "reservation."

Between 1823 and 1838 approximately 654 New York Oneida Indians, representing two small New York Indian clans, migrated west to the Green Bay, Wisconsin area. They were provided a 65,400 -acre "reserve" (100 acres for each Indian) out of what was once the Menominee Indian reservation, memorialized in the Treaty of 1838. The Menominee's are indigenous to the state of Wisconsin while the Oneidas are not. The Oneida reservation — if reservation is even the accurate term to use — no longer exists as it did 182 years ago. While all 21,000 acres of Hobart lie entirely within the former Oneida reservation, the other 44,000 acres of the Oneida's land are within portions of the municipalities of Green Bay, Ashwaubenon, Pittsfield and Outagamie County. Only the village of Hobart is 100% within the former reservation and, as long as Hobart thrives and flourishes, it remains a problem for the Oneidas as they have publicly boasted that their goal is to reclaim all 65,000 original acres. Hobart's current population of 10,000 residents includes approximately 2,500 enrolled tribal members.

Nonetheless, tribal and non-tribal peoples carved out livings with and next to each other from 1838 for the next 40 years or so. Oneida tribal members were allotted individual parcels of land *vis-à-vis* the Dawes Act in 1887. This suited the purposes of the U.S. government and most Oneidas since they wanted to participate in life and in government as their non-tribal neighbors did. The Oneidas wanted to farm and log their own land; they wanted to own and sell their own land. This unfolded so successfully that a 25-year transitional interval required by the Dawes Act was soon waived for most tribal members. Certainly, there were issues with regard to taxing, bank mortgages, schooling, and so forth, but progress had been made and the trajectory had been established. Individual tribal allottees were able to develop their parcels if so desired and, as it turned out in the majority of cases, sell their land. Land sales were made and property titles were exchanged multiple times. Success was such that by 1908 the towns of Hobart, Wisconsin (Brown County) and Oneida, Wisconsin (Outagamie County) had been incorporated, with Hobarts' first two town chairmen actually being Oneida tribal members. Assimilation was working and the human race was again doing what it always does without the "help" of government regulations or affirmative action: mixing and marrying. One need only look around the dinner table of todays' families to see this naturally occurring mixing pot.

However, thanks to the meddling of liberals and misguided Caucasian guilt, the relationship between the Oneidas and the Village of Hobart began showing signs of being strained in the 1930's when a minority of the Indians were encouraged and empowered by President Roosevelt's Department of the Interior to assert self-government once again.

Like the social engineers of today, Roosevelt's Interior Department foolishly thought that Indian culture and history could only be preserved *vis-à-vis* tribal government. With coaching from Roosevelt's lieutenants, the Oneida Tribe approved a tribal constitution in 1936, prior to which they were disorganized.

This 1936 date is important in that it is subsequent to the Indian Reorganization Act of 1934, which the U.S. Supreme Court held in 2009 to be the criterion before which recognized tribes can petition to have land owned in fee placed in federal trust on their behalf. Any tribe recognized post-1934 is not eligible for placement of land into trust. As of today, the issue obviously revolves around the definition of U.S. "recognition". This landmark U.S. Supreme Court case is *Carcieri v. Salazar* (2009).

The Village of Hobart maintains that without an Oneida tribal constitution until 1936 there was no tribe to recognize, and therefore the Oneidas shouldn't enjoy the ability to have land placed into federal trust on their behalf. Any and all contact prior to 1936 was simply to facilitate beneficial use and occupancy of reserved land until allotted to individual Indians. This was informal, incidental, or of no significance. The Treaty of 1838 was not with a tribal government, but rather executed on behalf of 654 individual Indians that had migrated from New York.

Mischief commenced, however, when gambling revenues — first legalized under the 1988 federal Indian Gaming Regulatory Act — provided the

Tribe with "discretionary" money to spend. Since 1988, gaming revenues have played an enormously large role in enabling the Tribe to purchase land — land for which it no longer has a real need. Mischief has morphed into malice, however. Since the 1990's, the Tribe has been earnestly purchasing as much available land as possible and then applying to the federal government to take it into federal trust on the Tribe's behalf.

One might say that this is no different than the federal government annexing land. Not so!

When one municipality annexes the adjacent municipality's tax base, the losing municipality is no longer obligated to provide its traditional services. Ideally this results in a net zero sum cost. However, successfully placing land into federal trust results in a "double whammy" to the taxpayer. First of all, and like an annexation, the land is removed from the property tax rolls and represents a loss in tax revenue to those local, county, school, and state taxing entities. Secondly, and unlike an annexation, these same taxing entities are still obligated to provide all of their traditional services nonetheless. Thus, there is a loss of revenue without a commensurate reduction in provided services: a double whammy. One way to look at this is that the federal government is fulfilling its trust relationship with the tribes on the backs of the locals — just one glaring example of dysfunctional federal Indian policy.

It is not just this loss of property tax revenue that has been an existential issue between the Village of Hobart and the Oneida Indian Tribe. The lost opportunity for economic development occurring from loss of municipally governed land becomes an incremental threat year after year.

A second issue between the Village and the Oneida Tribe — arguably even more important than the loss of tax base — is that Hobart has zero authority and jurisdiction over land placed in federal trust. (The same loss of jurisdiction and authority is also true of the county and state.) This means that all zoning ordinances, law enforcement, building permits, hunting/fishing regulations, burn permits, nuisance complaints, etc., etc. are irrelevant and not applicable on trust property.

A glaring example of this tribalism was the 1996 petition by the Oneida Tribe to be granted "treatment as a state" for purposes of regulating water quality throughout the original 65,400 acres. This was eventually denied by the EPA but could have resulted in the Tribe exclusively and ultimately influencing all — including non-tribal — farming operations throughout 100 square miles of Wisconsin dairy land. Furthermore, when trust parcels are patch-worked and checker-boarded over dozens of square miles, responsible and coherent economic planning and development becomes virtually impossible.

As stated earlier, the Oneida's goal is to reclaim all 65,400 original acres that were provided to them with compliments of Wisconsin's indigenous Menominee Indian Tribe and the federal government. It's more than interesting to note that the Oneida's notion of "original" stops with them but does not extend to the Menominee's who pre-dated the Oneida's in Wisconsin. If one accepts the Oneida's grievance that the white man interfered and interloped in "their" land here in Wisconsin, one must also accept that the Oneida's themselves interfered and interloped in the Menominee Tribe's reservation. The white man's settling was no less noble than was the Oneida's.

For many years, efforts were made by Hobart leaders to achieve a fair and amicable working relationship with the Oneida Tribe. Thus, 2004 marked the signing of the first-ever service agreement between the Oneida Tribe and the Village of Hobart. It was a three-year agreement which obligated the Tribe to reimburse the Village for municipal services provided to the Tribe in lieu of the lost property taxes from federal trust land.

A provision in the agreement forbade Hobart from objecting to Tribal applications to put more land into federal trust. If Hobart objected, they would forfeit the service agreement's annual payment. The Village Board didn't necessarily like the provision, but had been assured by the Tribe that they had no intentions of submitting any new fee-to-trust applications, at least during the term of the agreement. This turned out to be a lie. Within months, the Tribe submitted applications. Being disappointed, yet honorable and trustworthy, the Board did not object as required by the agreement and collected their annual payments. However, the annual payment due the Village in the third year was inexplicably delinquent. The Board had no assurance that they would even receive the annual payment. The Board concluded, at that point, that failure to remit the third annual payment was breach of the agreement and therefore they considered the agreement no longer binding.

The Board then objected to fee-to-trust applications at that point. The Tribe did eventually pay and wanted to negotiate to renew the agreement for the next term. The Village Board refused.

The Tribe obviously had never ever dealt with a party that told them that they could keep their money and that there were principles and intangibles which money couldn't buy. At that point the Village was threatened by the Oneida's chief legal counsel by telling Hobart leaders that they "should prepare for extinction." This entire episode was an epiphany for Hobart leaders in dealing with the Oneida Indians. The Village Board has not had another service agreement with the Tribe since.

While Hobart has never collected any service agreement payments since then, they have also enjoyed a freedom of choice and a sense of incorruptibility. These elected officials have come to believe that there should be service agreements, but that they should be nothing more than a recital of services provided and associated costs, much like an invoice. Any and all other conditions, e.g. fee-to-trust land applications and jurisdictional matters, should reside within other entirely different agreements if they reside at all. Meanwhile, the Tribe should be willing and intent on paying without condition for the services they receive, exactly as the municipality should be willing and intent without condition to provide the services — which we, in fact, do to this day — without compensation.

Given this set of circumstances between the Tribe and the Village, one must ask himself, "Who is the honorable party?"

The Village has objected on several grounds to each of numerous Tribal applications to place fee land (taxable land) into federal (tax-exempt) trust ever since 2007 and has been successful in doing so. The pace at which the Department of the Interior had been approving these applications has come to a complete halt ever since. We believe that this is due, at least in part, to the aforementioned 2009 U.S. Supreme Court's *Carcieri* decision. This is truly an existential issue for the village of Hobart as you can imagine the death spiral that would occur if taxable land were allowed to disappear over time.

The Village of Hobart has been singular in its approach to preserving property tax base, as well as its assertion of jurisdiction in the face of tribal challenges. Not only is the County (and the State of Wisconsin) a culprit in this slow-motion suicide, but so is the federal government.

At this point it is important to explicitly state that no one is painting the entire Tribe with one broad brush. There is a clear distinction between tribal government decisions and respect for tribal members, their ancestry and culture. Tribal governments lump government and members in one basket. That makes it easy to shout "racist" whenever one disagrees with a tribal government decision. Grievances are with the Oneida Tribal government while maintaining a great respect and admiration for the Tribe's history, culture and people, as we do with all other ethnicities.

We have also come to realize that the issues between Hobart and the Oneida Tribe lie primarily between two governmental bodies. Indian tribes enjoy sovereignty and a trust relationship with the federal government. This means that they may govern themselves and are protected by the federal government. When an Indian has a grievance against his tribal government and cannot realize a remedy therein, he will then often turn to the local government for such. Typically, these are problems that involve perceived injustices administered by the tribal police department, fraud, nepotism, or corruption within the Tribal government.

When coming to the Village of Hobart for some kind of relief or resolution, the plaintiff tribal members first want to be assured of anonymity. This stems from the fear that, if their grievance or their outreach to the Village government for remedy becomes known to tribal authorities, they may experience retribution such as a loss of job, housing, tribal services, or they may well be unenrolled from the tribe. Their fear is well-founded. The underlying problem is the degree to which tribal sovereignty has extended.

What was originally intended as federal protection of the Tribes from other governments (tribal sovereignty) has evolved — thanks in large part to federal courts — into oft-perceived internal miscarriages of tribal justice. Because of jurisdictional limitations, the local government often can only do so much. Alternatively, pleas for help to other quarters, particularly the federal government or individual members of Congress, are time-consuming, ineffective, or, more usually, fall on ignorant or indifferent ears. Knowledge of tribal history and understanding of federal court decisions are sorely lacking by these elected congressmen and bureaucrats.

Thus, these federal officials will stand behind tribal sovereignty and beg off of, or defer to, whatever the tribal authorities decide. Thus, with no checks and balances against tribal government, the aggrieved tribal member falls between the cracks of the tribal and federal governments. It's as if he has no representation on either side of the equation. The individual tribal member views himself as having been abandoned by the federal government and as though his Constitutional rights are nonexistent.

2008-2009 saw the Village of Hobart purchase undeveloped but prime real estate along its northern municipal border (State Highway 29). The Village was fearful of losing this potentially valuable commercial real estate and thus borrowed money to purchase the land. The land purchase was done during the nation's worst economy in 75 years and there was plenty of anxiety to go around. However, if the Oneida Tribe had purchased the land, you can guess what the outcome would have been — and there are no "do over's".

Fortunately, there were a couple of light industrial businesses and a reputable residential developer who saw an opportunity, assumed risk, and capitalized. We sold the necessary land to these parties and got the property and improvements on the tax roll. These 300+ acres have since become an indescribably successful site for almost $200M of new tax base, home for more than 1,000 new residents, and a couple of hundred new jobs. Hobart ranked as the fastest growing municipality in the State of Wisconsin in 2010-2014, on the basis of percent increase in population. Our strategy and hope in purchasing the land was to develop it and expand the property tax base such that it would compensate for the loss of property tax revenue due to tribal land going into federal trust. The strategy has succeeded beyond our wildest dreams; we are still developing.

Of particular note during this episode is the fact that the Oneida Tribe purchased an unbuildable, L-shaped piece of land perpendicular to the very route through which water and sewer infrastructure would be required to service this entire new tax base. This was done within months of the Village's purchase of the land and was obviously intended to obstruct any development and render our real estate purchase as stranded. Hobart condemned the "spite strip" for purposes of the public good and necessary infrastructure. The Tribe predictably sued the Village in federal court on the grounds that we lacked the authority to condemn tribal land. Our position was that, short of being in federal trust, the Tribal strip was owned in simple fee and, just like any other such land, was not immune to a government's power of eminent domain. The mere fact that it was owned by an Indian tribe made no difference. The Village prevailed.

Since this 2009 decision the Tribe has sued the Village several times, always over some jurisdictional issue. It's sad and unfortunate, particularly since it's all grounded on "institutional racism" fomented by the federal government.

It is no different than reparations, reparations to which there is no end, reparations which are so magnanimous that they are unsustainable over time, and reparations which, if discussed in the context of African Americans or any other ethnic group, typically enjoy no favor. It's unfortunate because in the eyes of the U.S. Constitution there are no races recognized other than the human race and the inalienable rights of all human beings.

The single most important reason that these tribal issues never seem to be resolved is the on-going victim mentality of the tribes and the all-too-willing federal government's subsidization of this dependence. There should be some embarrassment associated with claiming tribal sovereignty on the one hand and holding out the other hand for all of the federal government's subsidies, grants, programs, and tax breaks. Where is the tribal or individual pride to be found in that dysfunctional relationship?

In any given year, the annual operating budget for the Village of Hobart (population: 10,000) is approximately $4M. Juxtapose that to the annual operating budget of the Oneida Tribe of Wisconsin (national enrollment: 17,000) that ranges annually from $470 — $573 million. You do the math and tell me that this make sense.

Over twenty years ago, U.S. Senator Slade Gorton (WA) started a discussion about financial "means testing" all of America's Indian tribes. Of course, the Indian tribes in his state of Washington pooled their campaign donations in favor of his opponent at the next election cycle and Senator Gorton was defeated. Though his work on means testing has not progressed since his departure, his position remains workable and necessary. America's Indian tribes should be means tested in order to qualify for any federal monies. The Oneida Tribe of Wisconsin, for example, is among the most affluent tribes in the nation. That's wonderful and we wish them continued success. But there comes a point — defined as success — when a tribe no longer needs to be bankrolled, especially when there is so much discretionary tribal wealth being used to fund political officials and candidates, to lobby, to purchase land, and then to have it held by the federal government in beneficial trust — land which is no longer needed as it once was in the 18th and 19th centuries, or earlier.

Means testing would be a good first step toward ending tribalism as a governing system being escalated by federal leaders desiring to continuously expand the federal footprint that replaces state sovereign authority. Congressional legislation needs to be drafted and ratified that identifies criteria for success, defines the metrics, and terminates federal funding when a tribe has satisfied those criteria.

The federal government pours tens of billions of unaudited dollars from 29 federal agencies into 574 tribal governments with no accounting, no expectations, and no end game defined. Neither is there any reallocation of federal monies and benefits amongst the tribes themselves on a needs basis. This modus operandi would be disgraced within minutes in the private sector!

If means testing is the single most effective manner to check dysfunctional federal Indian policy's fatal effect on tribes and, subsequently, on the nation's economic health and state and local governments, then the second major shift that needs to occur is for the federal government to cease and desist with its reliance on tribal sovereignty. The federal government isn't so much respectful of tribal sovereignty per se as it is interested in hiding behind it to keep its fingernails clean and avoid dealing with sometimes messy tribal issues. This then often leaves the tribal member, aggrieved by his own tribe, without recourse of any sort. The individual Indian's Constitutional rights take second place behind oft-times corrupt or self-serving tribal justice.

The faux sovereignty shield behind which federal agencies and Congress hide also results in emboldening tribes to assert claims and rights which, for one good reason or another, they don't have. The time for change in federal Indian policy is long past due!

NOTE: Twenty years ago, a few citizens of Northern Idaho gathered to educate themselves and push back against tribal government overreach that threatened citizens and property owners around Coeur d'Alene Lake. The Tribe has consistently tried to take control of Northern Idaho waters, lake beds, private boat ramps, and numerous other items over which they had no authority. These citizens have stayed at the wheel and successfully protected their properties and rights. Their story of endurance and successes is a "how-to" for other communities experiencing tribal government takeover.

CHAPTER 23

The Long Game

By Pam Secord — Emida Valley, Idaho

Success requires adaptability and sticking-to-it-tiveness

In what seems like a lifetime ago residents of North Idaho learned that the Coeur d'Alene Tribe started legal action to take control of Lake Coeur d'Alene. At the time the residents did not believe this would even be possible. The State of Idaho assured the local population that they need not personally intervene because the state would take care of it and protect them. And, at the time the residents generally trusted their state government.

As details unfolded, a small group of residents who realized that property rights were in peril, together with their local legislative representative, met with the State Attorney General and voiced their concerns about the possible impacts to their property rights. They were dismissed. Our local government attempted to launch a legal challenge, even hiring a law firm to represent them, but they were locked out of the process by the court and State Attorney General's office.

U.S. v State of Idaho

When the first case, IDAHO I (U.S. v State of Idaho) was decided and was subsequently appealed by the state, reality started to sink in. We could see that the Tribe would continue their effort.

When IDAHO II went up to the Supreme Court it surely appeared that the state would win the case. The legal argument was sound and the state's brief was brilliantly written. However, a major flaw in the State of Idaho Attorney's preparation for oral argument was that they refused to talk to the affected citizens in the area. Had they not dismissed outright those brave citizens and local County Commissioners who tried to be heard, the outcome of the case could well have been different. And perhaps if the State of Idaho had employed an attorney who had good oral argument skills, the outcome could have been different.

Instead, when Supreme Court Justice Sandra Day-O'Connor asked, "what difference did it make who had control of the beds and the banks of Lake Coeur d'Alene, the Tribe or the State of Idaho" the response she received from the Idaho Attorney was, "Life jackets and fishing licenses." Justice O'Connor asked this question four times, likely with disbelief and hoping the attorney would give her some reason to vote in favor of the State of Idaho. Had the Idaho Attorney talked to the local citizens he would have been educated and able to articulate that the beds and banks of Lake Court d'Alene and the St. Joe River that feeds into it have been held in fee title by non-tribal people. And that there had not been any tribal presence on those lands in almost 100 years!

Those lands had been held by non-tribal citizens since they were sold or given homestead patents by the U.S. government with the allotment of the

Coeur d'Alene reservation in 1906. And almost all of the current banks and beds most impacted at the time of title transfer were not submerged at the time of non-tribal acquisition. Had the attorney spoken to the citizens he would have been able to tell Justice O'Connor that real people would have their property rights and lives turned upside down. The loss of IDAHO II in the Supreme Court in 2001 and the impacts that will forever be felt by area residents became the nexus for a small group of citizens to band together and fight back.

Lost was the trust that their state government cared about their property rights and interests as residents. Gone was the sense of community between tribal and non-tribal persons that had existed for many years.

The taking of land and property rights began with the Tribe using the Rails to Trails Act to claim the abandoned railroad along the lake. This land taken had been an easement by the landowner to the Railroad. Instead of it reverting to the landowner it was 'given' to the Tribes with the help of state and federal politicians. Local governments were either ignored or complicit by their silence. Citizens Against Rails to Trails (CART) formed to fight back, but their many hours of research and legal counsel failed.

But lessons learned helped with the next issue. Extortion like tactics were employed by the Tribe with the claim that permits for docks, boat houses and pilings issued to residents along the lake and river by the Idaho Dept. of Lands were no longer valid. The Tribe demanded that docks be removed or permitted with them. The state refused to intervene. What had been a lifetime permit of $100.00 paid to the State was now an annual fee of $100.00 with demands. Over the years the demands have expanded and increased. Permits for existing boathouses have been denied, with fees for permits ever increasing. The CART group had now become the North Idaho Citizen's Alliance (NICA) to reflect the broader issues that were being addressed.

Some landowners resisted, and the Tribe attempted to take them into Tribal court for not paying dock fees. Those who pled their case in the Tribal courts quickly found that the die was cast before they even spoke a word in their own defense. They were always guilty and fined. Most just gave up and turned over money and rights. In the community the fear became pay up or it will only get worse, until a few brave souls took on the Tribe, challenging their tribal court authority over non-tribal persons.

Using the judicial system instead of bullets

Wars have been fought over western water. Today, instead of bullets we use the judicial system. Our next challenge has been the longest, the most costly and the most important. In 2014 NICA once again expanded its mission. Taking on a new name, the North Idaho Water Rights Alliance (NIWRA) we began our biggest mission to date: the protection of the fundamental right to water. Western water rights are based on appropriation, or beneficial use, unlike water rights on the eastern half the USA which is appurtenant to the land. Western states have for decades been undergoing state water adjudications to determine how many water rights there are, and then legally adjudicate their ownership and priority of use in case of water shortages.

A significant case in which a non-tribal person prevailed was Coeur d'Alene Tribe v Johnson, in which NIWRA helped with legal research and locating a competent attorney. The Johnsons refused to appear in Tribal court where the Tribe had no legal jurisdiction. The Johnsons asserted that the land upon which the dock and pilings sat where part of the original land patent granted when the U.S. sold the land, but was submerged under an easement to Washington Water Power for overflow rights in the building of the dam. The Tribal court issued a decision in absentia finding the Johnson's guilty, fining them $17,400.00 in punitive fines and ordering them to remove their dock. The local Sheriff let it be known that he would not enforce the tribal order and that any entity attempting to remove the dock would be arrested, since the Tribe had no jurisdiction.

The basis for the Tribe's assertion was of course was the IDAHO II Lake case of 2001. *CDA Tribe v Johnson* case went all the way the Idaho Supreme Court, and in a landmark precedent-setting decision the court ruled that state courts may uphold a Tribal court decision *but they are not legally obligated to do so.*

The penalty fine imposed was vacated, with the court ruling that the civil penalty fell under the 'penal law' rule. This ruling holds that the courts of one country cannot enforce the punitive laws of another. With this ruling the Idaho Supreme Court overturned one of its own decisions, made 35 years prior, and recognized that tribal courts are a *foreign* court system. The ruling also left the door open for land owners to challenge the legal ownership of the beds and banks.

We could have more wins

More wins like this could be had but for one thing: lack of fortitude to stand and fight, and the willingness to band together financially. This case is just waiting for someone to take it to the next step and prove the rightful ownership of the submerged lands. The fight will be lengthy and expensive; a David and Goliath fight just waiting for right person and circumstances to take it further.

Tribes around the nation have been claiming vast quantities of water under federal water rights. Our saying is, "He who controls the water — controls the land." They use the Supreme Court decision in *Rosebud Sioux v Winters* ('Winters Doctrine') that says that the federal government had to have reserved a water right for Indians on reservations because, if not, the land would have been useless and uninhabitable. It also ruled that the amount of water was 'the minimum amount of water necessary to fulfill the purpose of the reservation'. This is also being applied to all reservations of public federal lands.

Also guiding water rights adjudications is the McCarran Act, which mandates that all water rights claims must be made and adjudicated by the laws of the state and in the state courts in which the rights are being claimed.

Thinking outside the box

In Idaho the founders of NIWRA learned from the experiences of those most negatively affected in the 27-year-long Snake River Basin Adjudication (SRBA). Ranchers learned the hard way. They were told by the State of Idaho that they did not have to file for their water rights — it would be done for them. They were told to file objections to conflicting claims or respond to challenges to their water rights.

These ranchers and cattlemen lost their 100-year-old water rights because they trusted their government, believing that the state would protect their rights. By the time they realized that they had been misled it was too late to be recognized in the court; they were locked out. An effort was launched to stop the carnage politically but it failed.

One lone ranch challenged the BLM taking of their 100+ years-old water rights. After a million-dollar legal battle prevailed it set a legal precedent in the *Joyce Cattle Company* decision. Although it bankrupted the company, many have since benefited.

We used that decision in the Coeur d'Alene Spokane River Basin Adjudication and had multiple water right claims by the BLM dismissed.

NIWRA model and strategy

NIWRA developed a model and strategy to protect our water rights from the water rights claimed in the basin by the Coeur d'Alene Tribe, the

USFS, and the BLM, all of which had significant impact on the residents' water rights in the adjudication basin.

We knew first and foremost that the State of Idaho was not going to advocate for the individual people impacted. We needed to be our own advocates. We knew that the Tribe and the US government attorneys on behalf of the Tribe and the other federal agencies had deep pockets and unlimited resources so we had to be smarter.

We knew we needed a good attorney with experience. We knew that beyond the legal court fight that we had a political component that could work for us or against us. And we knew that even within the State Legislature there were legislators on the Tribes "payroll" and needed to be watched. Success in any endeavor requires understanding your opponents — both seen and unseen — and understanding the challenges and/or limitations.

We knew it was coming

We had been involved under NICA in the last years of the Snake River Basin Adjudication, so we were watching. When we found a seemingly unimportant notice was published to get on the water court mailing list for notifications, we jumped on it. Relying on our political connections — developed over many years — we were kept informed on happenings at the Idaho State Capitol. And it really paid off!

Under NICA we formed a volunteer group which was then appointed to the local County Commissioners to assist in researching and advising on policy issues for coordination with state and federal agencies on natural resource issues. It was there that a fax arrived alerting us to an effort by a legislator on behalf of the Tribe to very quietly pass a resolution which would have taken their water rights claims out of the State court and put them into a dark room to be negotiated in secret between the state attorney general, governor, Tribe, Feds, and some legislators. Chills ran down the spines of everyone in the room. The Commissioners immediately set us to work stopping this effort.

And stop it we did, together with the many good State legislatures who fought to kill it. Countless hours were spent analyzing all the claims and informing key legislators so they could fully understand the extent of the claims, since they had been told it was nothing to worry about. Our legislators were stunned, feeling betrayed by the deception of the Tribe and Tribal friends in the legislative body. We spent many early mornings in conference calls helping to draft a new resolution that assured that all water rights claimants had the right to be at the negotiating table, and that the legislature had the primary role in oversight. This assured full transparency, with no backroom deals outside of the courts. Because there was an urgency to "do something" to address the Tribal demands, we effectively gave them "something" to choke on.

A coalition to share cost

NIWRA formed a coalition with two other citizens groups and two business entities to cost share our attorney. Idaho is blessed to have an experienced water rights attorney in Norm Semanko. As a native north Idahoan Norm understands not only the people of the area but the entities involved. He also has strong political ties in the State and Federal government. We could not have found a better attorney to represent us.

NIWRA, together with our partners, are affectionately referred by the court and state as the North Idaho Water Rights Group. We have been able to help guide all the agreements, framework documents, negotiations and all aspects of the process. The state has acknowledged that we are the 800-pound gorilla with a large number of voices. We have filed over 100,000 objections to the federal water rights claims. The state has recognized that no agreement will be signed off on without us.

When the state was protecting the rights of the residents, we praised them, and when they were going south, we knocked them upside the head with the legislative body. Once they understood that we were here, not going away, and had political clout, we started getting along great and became working partners in the effort. **We also never let down our guard with the State Attorney General's office.**

Building relationships and respect

It cannot be emphasized enough the importance of building relationships and respect within your legislative body and your state government. Know your enemy — both within and without. Be watchful. Be willing to be stay involved for the long term because these challenges are not flash in the pan affairs. Our organization has learned and evolved. We have taken on a multitude of issues, not limiting ourselves to one issue. And, although we have not always prevailed, our failures have taught us how to be more effective with the next challenge.

Our model has been effective

The Tribe and the other federal and state agencies had previously been effective of picking off citizen opposition, one at a time. They did not expect and were not prepared for an overwhelming coalition of citizens come together with one voice. We have successfully repelled efforts by the Tribe to have domestic and stock-water water rights held up from being decreed until their federal claims where decreed.

We have successfully defeated an effort by the Tribe to require domestic and stock-water claimants to prove how much they actually used each day. (Think water meters).

We successfully repelled the Tribes challenge to existing state issued water rights licenses by having the court decree that they should not exist and be nullified — a huge win for many. Since many individuals had their water rights challenged by the Tribe, requiring the individual to mount a legal defense in court or give up their existing issued water right, we assisted in building a funding model in which every one of our represented members had the Tribe' objections withdraw, assuring their water right being decreed by the court.

We also had a huge win in negotiations on in-stream flow water rights claimed by the USFS in the St. Joe River under the Wild and Scenic Act. The federal water right with a senior priority date could have been used to shut down the natural resource industry that supports the economy in small north Idaho rural communities. Our efforts led to a negotiated subordination of the federal water rights to all other water and land users in the river drainage. We settled 6 others and are close to settling the final remaining claims.

Big wins in court

We successfully had the court dismiss all of the in-stream flow water rights claims by the Tribe on streams and rivers outside of the reservation boundaries. In some cases, those claims wanted more than the stream flow during the dry part of the summer, which served some communities municipal water systems.

Our efforts were successful in having the industrial and commercial (current and futuristic) claims removed as federal reserved water rights with super senior priority dates. Those claims which are not within the initial stated purpose of the reservation must be filed and carry a priority date under state law.

Our biggest win was when the court rejected the Tribe's claim to determine the water level of Lake Coeur d'Alene. Had we not won, every water use from surface to ground water within and outside of the reservation boundaries, even crossing state lines, would have fallen under the control of the Tribe! The Tribe appealed to the Idaho Supreme Court, as did the State and our organizations. We have come away from these challenges in a good place to continue making gains in the next phase of water right quantification.

There is strength in numbers. Our NIWRA organization has accomplished much for our local area, and together with our partners we have made great strides in the broader water rights fight, both for now and for the future.

Sadly, many of our founding members have passed, but their legacy lives on. Now it is vital for the younger generation to get involved, stay involved, and continue protecting that which we have fought so long and so hard for. The impact of our citizen activist groups in this area will be felt and enjoyed for generations to come.

Of all tyrannies a tyranny sincerely exercised for the good of its victims may be the most oppressive.

— C. S. Lewis

Epilogue

In the Preface of this book, I spoke of Leonard Cohen's remarkable lyrics in his song, *Democracy*. When he penned *"I love this country but I can't stand the scene,"* it described my feelings exactly.

Imagine standing by a railroad track on a dark night and seeing a huge bright light coming down the track. There is no way to see how many cars are behind the engine. The bright lights are blinding us from seeing 574 tribal government cars roaring behind the engine and across the country. The bright *lights* are flashing terms such as *aboriginal rights, ancestral* and *traditional lands*, and *time immemorial*. This train and these terms are literally derailing state sovereign authorities, civil liberties of millions of American, and a cohesive, constitutional United States government.

Behind this enormous train is another large one, coupling up: that would be 400 additional Indian tribes awaiting their future taxpayer funded federal recognition, annual operating funds and tax-exempt casinos.

The country's future holds a cumulative possibility of just under 1,000 taxpayer-funded tribal governments, capable of purchasing elected officials at every level of American government, annually eroding state jurisdiction and tax revenues, and incrementally removing what is left of our **republic** form of government. This is the perpetual "scene" that our country cannot sustain, and I cannot stand.

Can you find a single word in our federal constitution that mandates special preference for one ethnicity, or the first, or second or third citizen over every other American, or even an American child born five minutes ago? Is there any authorization within the constitution enabling the federal government to continue or execute treaties with any American citizens?

Each of our fifty states have a fixed land base with a boundary that prevents a state from expanding its lands, governance or economic opportunity. "There shall be no state within a state," and yet federal government agencies implemented tribal "Treatment As States," (within a State) for any and all interested tribes. Tribal governments annually can and do expand their land bases within the fixed boundaries of multiple states. The tax-exempt tribal lands, tax-exempt tribal businesses, and tax funded operating budgets shift this huge annual tax loss — to be replaced as a perpetual burden on America's remaining taxpayers. Something is fundamentally wrong here.

The potential economic health of states is locked into guaranteed diminishing returns. The same is true for all taxpayers.

Another question: Among America's marvelous multi-cultures, how many are annually paid by other cultures to preserve themselves? Just one. Most cultures that respect and cherish their history, ancestry and traditions lovingly do so because it is their choice and personal responsibility, and the right thing to do, not because some government must pay them forever to exist.

Our federal and state governments have created a schizophrenic system that elevates as superior or preferential citizens enrolled tribal members while treating them as dependent incompetents, denying them their 14th Amendment, civil and constitutional protections. All other citizens are permanently indentured servants to finance this cruel hoax.

As earlier reported, I am of strong Cherokee ancestry and my spouse is Lemhi-Shoshone. My research would refute and eliminate all of federal Indian policy and allow American citizens of Indian ancestry to be restored of their full constitutional protections. I am certain that proud tribal members would not hesitate to continue to honor their culture and their past by choice and personal responsibility for the next seven generations.

Bear with me while I dream. I pray for a day when we not only cease, but disdain the use of such identifiers as Hispanic Americans, Black Americans, White Americans, Native Americans, etc. We are all simply Americans; no other identifier should have value or utility within government policy or decisions.

Wouldn't it be amazing if taxes, whether federal or state, were distributed based on one simple qualifier — Annual Household Income. This neutral, fundamental qualifier would render every single American equally eligible for assistance based upon an equal qualifier. Certainly, poverty thresholds would be established at federal and state levels, with distribution based upon number of American citizens in a household and their cumulative annual household income.

Ending federal Indian policy and using only annual household income as a neutral qualifier would produce several beneficial outcomes:

1. Current funding targeted to various ethnicities would be transferred and consolidated into one Poverty Support System available to every qualifying American citizen;

2. Federal and state agencies would eliminate specific sub-departments focused on ethnicities, transferring or down-sizing staff;

3. Federal and state governments would cease all future funding based only on ethnicity;

4. Federal lands held in title by the United States would be transferred to tribal governments that have reorganized themselves as nonprofit corporations;

5. All other non-federal lands within a state boundary, whether private or nonprofit, would be under the jurisdiction of the state;

6. Jurisdiction over all navigable waters of a state would be restored to state authority and control;

7. No further use of such pre-constitutional terms as *aboriginal rights, ancestral lands* or *time immemorial*, or any other term that renders the existence of the United States and its rule of law as irrelevant or secondary will be tolerated;

8. **All** Americans would be restored to equal protections and equal access to federal and state services, and;

9. America would be restored to *One Nation Under God* as intended by our Founders and the U.S. Constitution.

Yes, the above outcomes are but a dream for now, but they are the best tools for stopping a roaring race-based train from taking down our republic form of government — sooner than we might think. To be restored to

One Nation under God, with a mutual and equal respect for each other as Americans, is worth my every effort. So, America...

Sail On! Sail On!

Oh Mighty Ship Of State!

To the Shores of Need,

Past the Reefs of Greed,

Through the Squalls of Hate ..

Sail On! Sail On! Sail On!...

— Leonard Cohen

INDEX

www.ingramcontent.com/pod-product-compliance
Lightning Source LLC
Chambersburg PA
CBHW060320030426
42336CB00011B/1136